FINDING FREEDOM

"This book is for anyone who is
hurting and in need of healing"

REBECCA JOHNSON

Disclaimer

Please note that in preparing this work, I have attempted to describe events and locations, and in many instances, I have had to create conversations from my memories of what happened at the time. To protect their identity, I have changed the names of many individuals and places. I may also have changed or fictionalised certain identifying characteristics and details, including physical appearances, occupations, and places of residence.

This book is an honest, authentic story of my life. Some siblings may remember or be affected differently.

First published 2024

© 2024 by Rebecca Johnson

British Library Cataloguing in Publication Data

A CIP catalogue record for this book is available from the British Library.

ISBN:

Editorial and publishing services by

The Heritage Publishers Ltd

Cover Design by Jessica

CONTENTS

FINDING FREEDOM

'Delight yourself also in the LORD, and

He shall give you the desires of your heart.'

_____

- Psalm 37:4

FINDING FREEDOM

ENDORSEMENTS

Being able to closely witness the healing process described in this book has been a privilege. Rebecca's story is an encouragement to anyone seeking hope and freedom from life's darkest valleys.

Jed *(Rebecca's husband)*

A 'must read'.

Finding Freedom is a powerful story of healing and restoration.

Rebecca writes bravely, honestly, and thoughtfully about her life, providing enough detail to give an accurate and sensitive account of a dysfunctional family's dynamics while honouring each of the characters.

If you only read one book this year, make it this one.

Carolyn *(Rebecca's sister)*

Rebecca has poured her heart into the pages of this book, reflecting on her childhood, its impact, and her journey into healing through finding God.

Honest, open, and searching, her life speaks to us about resilience, courage, healing, and the power of trust in a faithful God, even when circumstances are seriously challenging and hard to understand.

Thank you, Rebecca.

Karen Loring *(Senior Leadership Team at Kingsland Church, Colchester)*

Finding Freedom is a memoir filled with some sadness, brutal honesty, and immense tenacity. A must-read for anyone needing that bit of hope that things can work out if you put your faith in God and don't give up when it gets tough. Brilliant read.

Sharon Broom

This is a story of redemption, rescue, and reality. Rebecca's prophetic call is to be the catalyst for brokenness. The journey has not been easy, but God's hand has guided her every step of the way. The pain she endured provided the building blocks for who she is today: helping disadvantaged people recover and leading them to the Father.

God bless you, Rebecca. You are a shining example of a woman with a road map. This book will save many from destruction and give them a clear vision of their destiny.

Penny Ianson
penny@propheticrevelation.co.uk

PREFACE

I am an ordinary person who suffered from depression that blighted my life. Then, one day, God invited me on a journey to find healing and wholeness. I knew it would be hard, but I decided to take the journey for myself and others - particularly the broken and hurting. I wanted to tell them about the God who heals broken people. With faith and lots of courage, I gave him access to the inner workings of my emotions and mind. It was scary at times, but I knew he would bring me through.

My story has not been written by a psychologist or psychiatrist. It does not contain any learned medical journals or papers but shares how God healed and restored my life. There were too many healing moments to list in this book, but I have recorded the main events that tie the story together, being quite explicit in places. I hope you can identify with my journey and that it can be an aid to your own healing.

This is my story.

FINDING FREEDOM

INTRODUCTION

My story starts when I was rushed to the hospital in an ambulance in April 2019. If you have ever been on a 999-emergency journey, you will know what I mean when I say it was like being in a sardine tin, rattling along at high speed. They were moving me to a specialist hospital for tests and procedures, which was all a bit of a surprise since I actually felt ok. I had a pain in my chest and felt light-headed, but I didn't think all this emergency treatment was necessary. But I was obviously in greater danger than I realised. Apparently, it was a heart attack.

As the ambulance raced along, sirens blasting, it all seemed like a bad dream. My husband was by my side, looking anxious but supportive as always. *How would I tell my family and friends? Should I even be worrying about them?*

At the hospital, I was moved to the emergency ward amid a dizzying blur of flashing lights and bleeping monitors. Firm but caring hands eased me into an unfamiliar bed. I was vaguely aware of people speaking comforting words as I anxiously took stock of this ugly intrusion into my ordinary day. Still thinking about the shopping and what else I was supposed to be doing, my mind struggled to focus on reality.

The pain in my chest continued, so they rushed me into an immaculate but featureless lab, which looked like a futuristic sci-fi movie set containing soulless robotic machines. Realising my life could be hanging in the balance, I signed a consent form before undergoing an angioplasty procedure - a special type of X-ray to check how blood flows through the blood vessels. It was all done very quickly, with hardly any time to take in, let alone understand the risks and forms. My arm was anaesthetised, and a line passed through an artery up into my heart. The consultants and nurses were robed and masked up top to toe. It was all very clinical.

The images came up on a computer screen.

'You have had a Spontaneous Coronary Artery Dissection,' the consultant said.

I tried to concentrate but could hardly take in what he was saying.

'It is a rare, serious condition that occurs when a tear forms in a blood vessel in the heart,' the consultant went on to explain. 'There's no need for stents, but you need to take medication and let it heal over time.'

It all sounded very frightening. 'Why did this happen?' I asked.

'It is quite rare, and not much is known about the condition,' He said. 'While not a classic heart attack, it's still classed as one, possibly caused by stress and high blood pressure.'

Thoughts raced through my mind. I wasn't aware of being stressed, and my blood pressure seemed under control.

Before long, I was back on the ward, wired up and wondering what would happen next. When the consultant arrived with a list of the medication, I cried. Statins, beta-blockers, blood pressure tablets, aspirin, blood thinners and something to help me digest them all! And for how long? I couldn't believe this was happening or that I was so ill I needed them all. Surely, there had to be some mistake.

My children arrived to visit me that evening. They looked worried, but their presence was reassuring. They left after a while, transporting with them my husband, who had been by my side throughout the ordeal. Once alone, I settled into the ward.

'Don't look so sad, love,' said the lady in the opposite bed. 'Once the nurses have put out the lights, you and I can go out clubbing!'

She kept my spirits up with her natural wit and banter, and we giggled for a few moments.

'What are you in here for?' I asked.

'My second heart attack.' She replied. 'I now have five stents where my arteries have narrowed. I am lucky to be alive!'

I pondered on her words. *Five stents!*

'Hello mate,' A voice said from across the room. 'I had a heart attack while working up on the scaffolding at the building site.'

I looked around. A young man was talking on his phone. He did not look more than forty. I gave him a little wave as we were all stuck in our beds and wired up to monitors. Opposite him, an elderly grey-looking man was dozing on his bed. His family had popped in one by one to see him.

Introduction

'We are going to take him down to the lab and fit a pacemaker.' The doctor said to his latest visitor as a nurse arrived to wheel him away.

I later found out he was ninety years old. There was an unspoken sense that we all knew we were lucky to be alive and were grateful for the caring nurses and modern technology that constantly monitored our condition.

When nighttime came, I hoped and prayed for sleep despite all the noise and wires attached to my arms and chest. After taking the cocktail of medications, I must have fallen asleep. At last, some rest.

Around 3am, I woke up feeling limp and lethargic with a dreadful headache. I wanted to press the buzzer but couldn't bring myself to sit up and find it. Something was wrong. The number 30 flashed on the monitor. *Was that my blood pressure or heart rate?* On cue, the buzzers went off, echoing like loud horns through the dimly lit ward.

Suddenly, a team of clinicians surrounded my bed. A nurse put stickers on my chest and held the paddles ready for resuscitation.

My life seemed to ebb away, but I felt surprisingly calm.

Was I dying?

I started praying silently as the team tried to locate a vein to medicate me. No one spoke to me, but the paddles hovering over my chest highlighted my critical condition.

'Shall we rush her into the lab?' One nurse asked.

The nurse in charge was trying to fit a fresh cannula into my arm. 'No, wait a moment,' She said before putting some medication through the newly inserted cannula.

'She's responding,' one nurse said after what felt like an hour but was only several minutes.

There was a collective audible sigh of relief around the bed.

I started feeling a bit brighter, and the headache subsided.

As quickly as they had rushed to my bedside, the team left the room.

The lady in the opposite bed had been woken up. 'Are you ok?' she asked me in a hushed, sombre tone. 'I thought we had lost you!'

Her words sent a chill down my spine. I had just had another brush with death.

No one explained what had happened to me that night. The staff were busily unaware of the impact this experience had on me.

Introduction

I tried to sleep, but my tangled thoughts and feelings of anxiety allowed no rest. I had been much too busy in the past to give imminent death any real consideration. Now, in the hospital bed, I started seeing horrible images of myself looking down at my own funeral. It was heartbreaking to imagine how my children would feel as my coffin was carried.

A few nights later, I was moved to a side ward with less monitoring, but I was so scared to go to sleep that I asked my husband to stay in my room to keep a check on me. I hoped he would sit by my side, but he became tired and lay down on the floor by the window. The nurse who came in to do the final checks was surprised to hear someone snoring on the floor.

'Can he stay tonight, please?' I asked hopefully.

'I will ask the nurse in charge,' came the disapproving reply, but she reappeared a few moments later with a blanket and pillow.

Over the next few days, my anxieties settled down, and my husband returned home between visits. Now, in a quieter side room, I had plenty of time alone to reflect. The reality and certainty of death stayed with me, luring me into a new perspective. Many things that had filled my mind and the endless rushing around chasing material things now seemed pointless. This was a real dilemma, and I needed to talk to someone.

I asked to see the hospital chaplain. A down-to-earth middle-aged lady with a cheerful, comforting smile promptly arrived at my bedside.

'My name is Sandy.' she said. 'You asked for the hospital chaplain?'

'Thank you for coming to see me. I had a horrible experience last night and think I could have died.' I said immediately.

'Tell me what happened.' she said, pulling up a chair to sit beside me.

All I could think about was the paddles hovering over my chest. I had seen ominous scenes like this on television.

'The nurses were holding resuscitation paddles over my chest in the middle of the night. I am not ready to die yet.' I said, trying not to shake as I relived the trauma. 'I am shocked to think it could happen now. I have spent my life rushing around trying to fit in so much, and suddenly, it all seems pointless!'

The chaplain didn't say much but listened attentively. Her warm smile was reassuring.

'All I want to do now is slow down and spend some time with my family,' I continued. 'When you are doing so much and not even absorbing any of it, it becomes pointless.'

'I will pray for you,' Sandy said. I bowed my head, and she immediately said a brief but impactful prayer. Over the next few days, we spent several hours chatting through my brush with death and working through my tangled thoughts.

As the days passed by, I thought deeply about the many ups and downs. It was no surprise I ended up in the hospital bed – my life had not been easy. The events flashed before me like a video: Homelessness, bankruptcy, divorce, remarriage, and parenting seven children, but the most stressful had to be my endless battles with my mental health and the bouts of depression that plagued me like a shroud of death.

Eventually, I returned home after eight days in the hospital and, after a lot of rest, resumed my life. However, I was never the same. I no longer had the same priorities. I had to slow down and rest, something I had always found hard. Over time, I began to enjoy the slower pace and the time to sit, reflect, and appreciate simple things.

So, I made a decision - on coming through this heart attack, I would write my testimony of how Creator God healed me. I felt an urgency to write down my amazing story to help others on a similar path. It would be a waste to die without leaving a legacy behind.

Life would have turned out differently had I not been rescued and healed. God completely restored my brokenness and gifted me with a rich, wonderful life.

My story is funny, incredible, full of adventure and fun, miraculous and beautiful. It's the account of a person who, having failed to find happiness, allowed her Maker to heal, mend and give back her life as he intended it to be.

EARLY MEMORIES
1960-1988

Holidays on the farm

Childhood memories are few and hard to recall. So overwhelming were certain experiences that I locked them away in a mental box.

My earliest recollection is of me clinging to my mother at the school gate on my first day at primary school. She was busy chatting to other mums, prizing me off her legs, while my tummy churned with anxiety, a little girl desperately wanting Mum's comfort in an unfamiliar world.

I also remember not liking the bottles of milk we were made to drink at infant school because of their unpleasant, sour aroma. *Yuk!*

My parents died in 2017. While sifting through their belongings, I discovered a collection of old photos that triggered more childhood memories, particularly of our lovely family holidays. Dad being a teacher meant we could go away in our caravan for the entire six weeks, so we stayed on a farm in North Devon, where his family lived.

We usually left at the crack of dawn to avoid heavy traffic. There was no M25 or useable motorways in those days, so the only way to get to the west country was driving right through London. We kept stopping at traffic lights, and it seemed if you got caught in one, you got caught in them all!

Once through London, we had the long drive to Devon, always stopping off for a great fried breakfast in the caravan.

Five children and a golden retriever dog all packed into the car. With no seat belts in those days, we must have sat together in the back seat. I recall being silly with my sisters and holding up our socks at the window to other drivers. We thought it was hilarious!

It must have been a slow old drive with a large caravan in tow. The car struggled at the Devon hills, so we all got out and walked, leaving my dad to pull the caravan alone.

As the middle child in our large family, I had three sisters, two of them eight and three years older and one who was two years younger than me. Then, my brother came along eleven months later. We, the three youngest siblings, were called 'the little ones' and played together.

My favourite thing was staying on the farm and playing in the haystacks. I can still smell the hay, the comforting scent of a sun-soaked meadow. It was such fun getting lost among the hay bales, going with the farmer to bring in the cows (my favourites were Buttercup and Daisy) for milking, followed by a soak in an old tin bath in the farmhouse kitchen.

There were beautiful rural walks around the farm, with stunning meandering streams, rivers, and endless fields full of animals and wildlife. Wildlife was rich in those days, with bees, dragonflies and beautiful coloured butterflies fluttering in the summer breeze. I would catch the butterflies in jars (of course, I let them out again). It was fun, and there were so many to catch.

Staying on the farm and exploring the Devon countryside sowed seeds in my life and gave me a taste and hunger for a farming lifestyle.

Family dynamics

My father was brought up in the West Country and had a twin sister. His father died of TB when my dad was sixteen. Dad also caught it and was hospitalised for twenty-two months. I recall him saying he saw others dying around him, which must have been quite traumatising. Eventually, a doctor suggested he try some new medication being researched. Dad agreed, becoming one of the first to recover and go on to lead a healthy life. The medicine was Penicillin.

Dad trained to be a secondary school teacher, settling in Essex, where he met and married my mum. He taught in the same school all his life and became head of the lower school.

He was a tall, imposing man with a severe Victorian attitude. He liked to be in control as a proper disciplinarian and head of the house and wanted to be seen as a respectable head teacher with a successful family. What others thought of him was important. In the Victorian era, children were seen and not heard, and that was how he liked it! Dad knew how to whistle, and he had one whistle for the dog and a different one for us children. When he whistled, we had to come running, or there would be trouble.

He often fell into rages, mostly about silly things, and whenever we were naughty, we were disciplined. For extreme behaviour, it was caning with a stick. This might sound barbaric, but caning was widely used in those days. Dad was also the teacher responsible for caning at the school, so he was used to this type of discipline.

One day, an orange went missing from the fruit bowl. Enraged, Dad whistled for everyone and lined us up like suspects.

'Who stole the orange?' He bellowed, red-faced and fuming.

I was terrified and desperately wanted someone to own up since the culprit would likely get the cane. When no one owned up, I secretly wondered if he had eaten it himself and then forgotten.

Everything revolved around what Dad thought and wanted, and I learned to be quiet and toe the line. You had to be careful voicing an opinion, especially if it differed from his. He not only extinguished whatever resisted him, he could never be wrong about anything and would criticise and judge anyone who didn't meet his high expectations. Dad didn't forget or forgive anything and had a long list of those who had crossed him over the years.

Mum lived to please him and became a slave to his needs. If she objected or voiced another idea, he engulfed her in a tsunami of anger. She could never win. I hated hearing them argue as Mum was frequently crying and upset.

Dad's terrifying moods often sprang out of nowhere, like when they played bridge with their posh friends downstairs in the dining room. These were evening events, and I was confined to my bedroom. The moment the friends left, he exploded like a volcano.

'You ridiculous woman! Why did you play that card!'

His shouting went on for hours while I lay awake in my bed, too frightened to move as Mum sobbed and pleaded with him. The rows went on all evening and sometimes into the next day. Despite all this, he hated being alone and was deeply dependent on Mum, and as they grew older, I noticed the insecurities behind his head of the house image. He could not live without my mum's constant companionship and help.

My sister and I slept in a loft room. It was fun being hidden right up in the top of the house with our own washing facilities. We often lay awake at night in our two single beds, whispering, laughing, and playing jokes on each other.

Sometimes, I planned to run away.

'Let's escape to the Martello Towers,' I said. 'I can sneak out the back door when everyone's asleep, get my bike from Granny's and then go!'

The Martello Tower is a dreary little fortress on the Essex coast, but to my young mind, it was somewhere to take refuge.

I lay awake, planning how to get there and what to take on the picnic. I never went, but it was great to plan.

Mum was from a loving and caring home. I don't remember her getting angry or telling us off too much. Because she worked when we were little, we had a cleaning lady. Looking back, I don't know how Mum managed to work full-time.

I don't remember any one-to-one times with my parents; there was probably too much to do and too many of us. However, the beauty of a big family is having siblings to play with, and we kept ourselves entertained. Home life could be chaotic, but Dad ruled with a harsh rod and kept us all in order.

Mum and Dad provided well for our material needs. They took us out to interesting places like museums and country walks. We also went on lovely holidays in the South of France and Spain when we were teenagers.

My granny and grandad lived around the corner and played an instrumental part in my life as I was growing up. They had a lovely one-acre garden and spent their retirement years making it look splendid. Passers-by stopped to look at Grandad's wonderful display of dahlias by the front path. They grew all their own fruit, and I have lovely memories of helping with the fruit harvest.

Every week, Granny had me over on my own after school for tea. I loved it! We had one-to-one time where I felt cherished and loved. She was also religious, and I sang with her in the church choir. She introduced me to Christianity and the love of gardens, both of which sowed seeds in my heart for later in life.

Meanwhile, Dad found it hard to share any feelings of love with his children, and he parented from an emotional distance. Love was never talked about, and feelings were never expressed, discussed, or understood. Instead, he seemed challenged by women's emotions.

Whenever Mum shed tears during an argument, he was infuriated. 'You stupid emotional woman!' he would shout furiously, making her cry even more. He even hated women crying or shouting on the television.

'Turn off that television! It's stupid emotional women!' was frequently heard in our house.

When we went on long car journeys, Dad used the opportunity to teach me, sometimes about history or geography, but he also taught me that it was a weakness to be ruled by my heart instead of my head.

I knew that Mum cared and loved me but was unable to express that love living under Dad's control. Emotionally, I was left to my own devices, and I suppressed my feelings, believing it was stronger to function without them.

Within this environment, I had no idea what my emotions were. There was nowhere to express myself; my tears were bottled up and let out on a lonely pillow at night. Little did I know that depression was developing within my soul as these dynamics took their toll on me. The lack of emotional nurture left me feeling abandoned, resulting in depressive episodes later in life that I couldn't control or understand.

Although I grew physically, my emotions were stunted and filled with horrible, unexpressed pain and confusion. When I tried to get on with life as an adult, deep depression raised its head again and again, popping up for no apparent reason and tainting everything I did.

Growing up

Despite being bright and intelligent, I struggled during my school years. Dad thought education was everything to be proud of and was not happy unless we got A+ grades. It wasn't easy, but I managed to pass my eleven-plus exams and go on to a grammar school. I attended secondary school in the next town by public bus.

We lived near the school where Dad taught, and I endured a lot of bullying from the local youngsters calling out, 'Teacher's daughter!' as I walked to the local shops. I dreaded leaving the house. I made several friends whom I kept throughout my school years, but I never confided in any of them about my home life. I was embarrassed by Dad's reputation as a harsh teacher and told my school friends that my father was a bus driver.

When I was fifteen, the pressures of home life and exams became overwhelming. One evening, I took a large handful of paracetamol tablets from the bathroom cabinet, swallowed them, and slumped on the bed, wondering whether I would wake up. Sleep came very quickly, but I woke up in the morning, remorseful for taking such a risk. I tried telling Mum I had taken the tablets, hoping for some support, but she seemed too preoccupied.

My parents had full-time jobs, and Dad worked most evenings in a youth centre. When he wasn't home, we took the opportunity to let off steam and let rip at each other.

'Have you stolen my make-up?' I would growl at my sister.

'Get out of my room!' I would yell to the younger siblings trying to hide in my room. 'I hate living here!' It often got very heated as we swore and shouted at one another. This was the only way I knew to release the pent-up tensions and emotions.

Dad had high academic expectations and made me revise in my bedroom for eight hours a day during exam time, but my results were never good enough. When I started in the school's sixth form, he insisted on my retaking some O Levels while tackling three A Levels. It was so overwhelming that I started withdrawing from my lessons and hiding in the school toilets.

An observant teacher eventually notified the headmaster, Mr Brunt, who was quite scary. He was red-faced, rather fat and round, and always in a hurry.

He summoned me into his office and peered over his round spectacles at me.

'Are you attending any lessons?' he asked, not taking his eyes off me.

I broke down. 'I can't cope with my lessons.' I sobbed, rummaging around in my school bag for a tissue. 'I just can't keep up!'

'According to the school records, you have not attended any lessons for weeks.'

I stared at him blankly. *What could I say?*

He flipped through some papers on his desk, stopped and peered at me again. Then he sat back against his creaky chair. 'Rebecca, I believe you must be here through choice,' He said. 'Why choose these subjects when you can't keep up with them?'

I had no reply to that, either. I couldn't tell him that it was my father's wish that I study and not mine.

But Mr Brunt was a discerning man. He read the situation and asked me a surprising question. 'Would you prefer to be at work?'

The thought had not occurred to me, but as soon as he said it, I felt a weight lift off me.

'I… I think so,' I said hesitantly. 'But my dad may not let me.'

It was easy to get a job in those days; there were no complicated forms or CVs.

Mr Brunt picked up the telephone sitting on his huge wooden desk. 'How do you fancy a job in a bank?'

I couldn't believe we were having this conversation!

'I will give it a try,' I said, trying not to get too excited. Something within me started to come alive. Hope, perhaps?

With one phone call, the headmaster got me a job as a bank clerk at a local bank.

Then he phoned my dad to tell him, and I heard him say, 'Hello, it's Mr Brunt here.

I didn't hear my father's reply, but Mr Brunt continued.

'I am calling to let you know I have just found a job for Rebecca.' He went on to explain his reasons while I sat there open-mouthed. 'She will be starting at the bank next week and will not be returning to school.'

I sat there, dazed at what had just happened. Then, the thoughts flooded my mind. What if Dad made a fuss when I got home? Would I get into trouble? Would Mum get yelled at for this? The scenes flooded through my head until I started panicking at the thought of going home.

Surprisingly, he never said a thing, and that was how, at 17, I started my first job. I loved every minute of it.

Moving out

As children, my father's discipline was enough to keep us in order. But getting older and trying to find our own way caused countless arguments. He would disapprove of a boyfriend for no reason and demand that the relationship end, and he often insisted on my attendance at last-minute family meals despite having other plans.

Mum tried to stick up for me but always gave in.

'Just keep the peace.' She pleaded. 'Your father will make me ill if you don't do as he says.'

This tormenting cycle of control was how the family operated and how Dad controlled us all into adult life.

Dad had carved an emotional landing pad of guilt into the family and always used this manipulation to get his way.

'You wicked child! Look what you have done to your mother.' or 'You are making your mother ill' was another well-used expression to lever control. Seeing Mum upset at his bullying was too much to bear, so I repeatedly conceded.

With all this going on, sadness festered in the deeper dungeons of my mind, and I was quietly desperate to escape my home environment. Once I was old enough, I started dating and enjoyed every minute of the attention.

After receiving several marriage proposals, I said yes to a young man in 1978 and started planning to move out and get married. Marriage had to be done the traditional way; there was no living together beforehand. We saved up to purchase our first home, and the wedding followed in 1981.

Planning the wedding was easy; however, adjusting to married life was harder than I imagined. For one thing, I was used to the hustle and bustle of a big family. In contrast, life was now relatively quiet, which I enhanced with alcohol and lively parties. Nonetheless, it was wonderful to have flown the nest, and I could now truly let my hair down.

All my siblings left home and moved to other parts of the country, and my parents bought another house in the West Country, where they spent much of their time. However, despite the geographical distance, if Dad was around, I still had to live up to his expectations. His occasional visits left me on tenterhooks, terrified of doing something wrong and triggering his outbursts.

About a year later, family life began, and four beautiful children were born. Two gorgeous girls, eighteen months apart, my son after two and a half years, and another beautiful daughter seventeen months later. Pregnancy and becoming a mother released a torrent of love and fulfilment I didn't know existed in me. I loved the fluttering and little kicks from the babies growing inside me, and pushing the pram with them all tucked up inside made me feel proud, needed, and wanted, filling the barren emotional gaps in my life. Bringing up my little family was my greatest achievement, and I am immensely proud of them all.

In those days, mental health conditions came with a terrible stigma, and people with such illnesses were considered fit only for mental institutions. There was no education; instead, people laughed and would tell you, 'the men with white coats' were coming to take you away. It was not something anyone would admit to.

During my teenage years, I was emotionally up and down like all hormonal and moody teenagers, but after my third baby, I suffered from post-natal depression. My mood was low, and I struggled to cope. Not knowing how to talk about my feelings, I ploughed on and waited for the symptoms to pass.

HELL, AND A HARD PLACE 1988-1992

Life on a downward spiral

Being married with four little children can be stressful, but I loved having mine together. They were my life, and I loved being a full-time mum. I was now living in a lovely country house and sharing a lifestyle with friends and family; however, my life was periodically blighted by depression.

In 1989 and 1990, there was a recession in the housing market, and the value of our house fell dramatically. Then, the marriage fell apart, and I became a single parent. A marriage breakup is hard to bear, especially when children are involved. Deeply anxious for the welfare of my now two, three, six and seven-year-old children, I cried myself to sleep at night after tucking them up in bed. In addition, home now felt like an unmanageable empty shell, and I could not maintain its upkeep.

After a series of court hearings, the judge ordered the house to be sold because, among other issues, the mortgage was now bigger than its value. I tried working part-time but with two children still under school age, it was a lost cause. I had no means of earning an income and kept drawing on daily reserves of hope and adrenaline.

Not long after, a letter from the bank arrived summoning me to court to repossess the property. I was in a world I knew nothing about. My parents had retired to the West Country, so I only had their phone support. My siblings were busy getting on with their lives, and friends kept their distance for fear of taking sides. I had a few friends of my own, but the situation was beyond their realm of support. I felt very much alone.

Court was a heartless place. Despite my requests to stay in the house for Christmas, the bank representative wanted me out, so the judge set a date and approved my eviction for two months' time, just before Christmas 1992.

Where would I go?

I rang the Citizens Advice Bureau and was told to inform the council and benefits offices that I would soon be homeless.

With three children now at school, I put my youngest daughter, Georgina, in the pushchair and headed for the town centre. The council building looked old and in need of repair, with people coming and going, all looking downcast. Inside, everyone's desperate looks, sunken eyes and ragged clothes spoke volumes. I had not mixed with people like this before.

Many seemed angry and kept shouting about their situations to the ladies behind the desk. Some asked for loans to buy cookers and other essentials, and those who were homeless pleaded for housing. But the council staff barely made eye contact. It felt like they treated these desperate people with suspicion, not compassion. There was little privacy; we all heard everyone's dilemmas.

I was eventually summoned to the front desk, behind which sat a weary-looking woman with grey roots showing through her brown hair. Perhaps she hadn't had time to dye her hair or no longer cared how she looked. Her face carried the same tired, suspicious expression as her colleagues. I settled down and attended briefly to Georgina.

I handed over my court paperwork.

She skimmed through it for all of thirty seconds before looking at me. 'Good morning. How can I help you?' Her face belied her words.

'I was asked to come here for help.' I said, holding back my tears. 'The bank is repossessing my house in two months, and my four children and I have nowhere to live.'

The compassion I expected did not cross her face even for one moment. Maybe she'd heard countless stories like mine.

'We haven't got many houses, you know.' She began before launching into a barrage of questions that made me feel I was under interrogation.

'Can you live with your parents?'

'No, they live in the West country.'

'Where is your husband?' By now, she was not even looking up from her paperwork.

'He doesn't live with us anymore.' I said tearfully.

'Can I see evidence of this?' She said curtly.

I flicked through my bag, trying to find the court paperwork, all the while thinking, *She doesn't believe me.*

I wasn't at all prepared for this harsh new world where people would be so suspicious.

'Here it is.' I handed her more court papers.

She gave them another cursory glance. 'You might be better off renting privately,' She said studying the papers on the desk.

'How can I afford that?' The tears I had tried to stop started streaming down my face.

I think she realised she had broken me with her intense questioning because she finally made her first proper eye contact.

'We cannot guarantee you a home. You may have to go into bed and breakfast accommodation as a temporary measure,' She told me with a small smile. 'It all depends on what is available at the time of repossession.'

I guess she was trying to look sympathetic, but her smile just looked practised and false.

I wanted her reassurance. 'Where will I end up?'

She gave me none. 'Fill in this form with your housing location preferences, but you will have to accept whatever is offered at the time.' She said bluntly.

Reality dawned on me - I had no control over anything. I returned home and carried on bringing up my family, hiding my concerns from my children. Deep inside lurked a dark foreboding of the future.

Because of the distance, my parents could not offer practical help, and there was no one else I could turn to.

My inner strength and love for my children kept me going, but I often lay awake at night, desperately unhappy and deeply troubled, wondering what the future held.

Finding a new start

During this time, my children attended a holiday club at the church in the next village. On one occasion, when I picked them up, a lady introduced herself as Angela.

'We are starting a new enquirers group.' She said, smiling at me. 'Would you be interested?'

'Maybe, if I have the time.' I replied in a non-committal tone. I was not interested in a stuffy old church or how it related to my current predicament.

'Let me have your phone number, and I will give you a ring when it starts,' She said enthusiastically.

I scribbled my number on a piece of paper, handed it to her and hurried off.

The phone rang a few weeks later. 'Hello, Rebecca. It's Angela. The enquirers group starts next Tuesday at my house. Are you still interested?'

I still didn't want to go but found myself agreeing to attend. Not knowing how to get out of it, I asked my neighbour to look after the children on Tuesday.

My first visit surprised me.

'Hiya!' A lady in a fashionable pair of tight jeans and a puffy top said as I walked in. 'My name is Rhonda. Have I seen you at the school gate?'

We shook hands.

'Do your children go to St Helenas school too?'

'Yes! I thought I recognised you.' She replied, beckoning me into a lounge where the seats were all laid out in a semi-circle. 'You can sit next to me if you like.'

The comforting aroma of baking permeated the house, and a lady approached us from the kitchen carrying a tray of cakes and hot drinks.

'Help yourselves,' she said, putting the tray on a large table in the middle of the room.

I grabbed a cup of tea and sat down next to Rhonda. 'Do you go to the church, Rhonda?'

'Yes, I have been going there for about ten years,' she replied. 'I am also one of the helpers on tonight's course.'

Others arrived looking a little anxious, but the helpers' genuine hospitality soon put them at ease.

Someone called Brian was smoking a cigarette outside the back door, which got my attention. Christians were supposed to be out of touch I thought, often wearing frumpy clothes. These people seemed a bit different.

Once all eight of us were seated, there was a time of introduction. There were six new people, plus Rhonda and Angela. Two other ladies bustled in and out, making drinks.

As the evening progressed, we were invited to talk about our experience of Christianity.

When they came around to me, I thought back to my childhood.

'My granny often took me to church,' I began, fidgeting slightly in my chair. 'It was not remarkable, just an old-fashioned traditional service and probably where I got my first impressions.' I finished with a small laugh.

Some of them nodded and seemed interested, so I continued.

'I remember singing in the choir and having weak tea and Rich Tea biscuits. The experience was mundane, but it gave me a belief in God, even if I wasn't following him. I have always believed in God, just in case.' I added.

Angela gestured to the next person, who happened to be Rhonda.

'I have been a Christian for about twelve years. I used to think being good was how you got to heaven, but then I heard that Jesus is the only way and that He died to forgive my sins.' She paused for a while before continuing. 'I know three things for a fact: we are all sinners who need forgiveness; Jesus has changed my life, and I don't know what I would do without him.'

I sat there, slightly stunned. I had never heard Jesus talked about in such an intimate way.

Then it was Brian's turn. 'My mum took me to church as a kid, but I did not give my life to Jesus until six months ago,' he said. 'I am on a bit of a journey. There's a lot to sort out in my life, but Jesus helps me step by step.'

How fascinating! I listened to the stories, and the penny began to drop. Following God wasn't automatic: you had to ask Him into your life and turn away from wrong things.

This is what repenting of sins and being born again meant. God would wash all your sins away and give you a new start.

As soon as we finished, Angela walked over to me. 'I would love you to have this,' she said, handing me a book.

It was a Bible.

'Oh, that's very generous of you,' I said, wondering why they would do this. 'I will return it next week.'

'It's yours to keep.' She said with a lovely smile. 'There is a helpful index at the front if you don't know where to start reading. See you next week?'

I nodded and headed for the door.

At home, I eagerly flicked through its pages, and soon, the stories started to come alive. Over the next few days, I read the verses on anxiety, needing guidance and hopelessness, and slowly realised that God wanted to help me. I could not put the Bible down. I read it on the loo, in the garden, everywhere. Gradually I began to understand the stories I was told as a child.

There was hope – God loved me. He could help me.

Never having experienced a father's love left a gaping void in my life, but it could be filled by the love and care of Father God. There could be no doubt. It was right here, in writing! This was an amazing time of transformation for me.

The enquirers' group must have been so pleased with my progress because I returned the following week full of questions and zeal!

As they explained how Jesus Christ died on the cross to take away our sins and reconcile us to God, I realised there was far more to Christianity. I decided to ring my brother

Tom, who was a Christian, to share what I had been learning.

'Hello, Tom. How are you doing?' I said as soon as he picked up the phone. Before he got a word in, I carried on. 'I've been going to an enquirers group at the church, and they gave me a Bible. I've got so many questions!'

'That's great news!' he said when I finally paused for breath. 'Why don't you come to our church this Sunday? We have a special guest service.'

'That's a long way to travel for church,' I said hesitantly. It was a sixty-mile round trip.

'Well, come here for tea first,' he said quickly. 'You can leave the children with Grace, and I will take you to the service.'

It was nice to catch up with my brother and his wife. They had been Christians for years and were always kind and pleasant. Once the children were settled with Grace, Tom drove me to the service. He was playing the keyboard that night, so he left me to find a pew. I looked around and had that funny butterfly feeling in my stomach. The church was full of people, young and old, all smiling and seemingly full of joy.

'Hi there,' said a lady from the pew behind me. 'Are you new? I haven't seen you before.'

'Yes, this is my first visit,' I replied, feeling awkward. 'My brother Tom is playing in the worship band.' I gestured towards the stage.

'I do hope you enjoy the service,' she replied before sitting back in her chair. The band continued to tune their instruments.

I had never seen drums and guitars at church. This was a far cry from the traditional organ and dreary songs of my childhood experience. They looked more like a rock band.

As if responding to an invisible command, the band and congregation burst into a beautiful song with lyrics full of love that melted my heart. These people were so warm, demonstrating a kind of love I had not experienced before.

When the singing ended, the vicar, a middle-aged man in jeans and a pair of trainers, got up.

'I used to be a salesman,' he said. 'I loved making money and was really good at it. Then one day, God asked me, 'Will you be a salesman for me?'

He spoke in such a relatable way that I was intrigued. '*Wow! Fancy hearing God speak like that!*'

'I knew God was calling me into ordained ministry,' He continued. 'He wanted me to preach and teach the gospel, a different sort of selling. The goal was no longer money, and I would have to leave my materialistic lifestyle behind.'

As he spoke, I wondered about my own life. *Perhaps God wanted me to do the same?*

'When I told my wife, she was furious,' The vicar carried on. 'She loved shopping and treating herself, and now I was leaving my job! She did not want to be a vicar's wife.

'But God said to me: "I don't force anyone to do anything." He showed me a roller coaster, saying, "You can stop and get off anytime you want to. You always have a choice."'

I liked the picture of a roller coaster. That was my life.

The vicar continued. 'After some time, we began to realise this would be an exciting new journey. I left my highly paid job and lifestyle and never looked back. God has given me back more than I gave up, and my life is fuller than I could have imagined. Some friends didn't like me becoming a vicar, but I now have numerous new friends.'

I liked and understood his down-to-earth approach and knew God was also calling me to make a serious and proper commitment to follow him.

At the end of the service, the vicar asked anyone who wanted to make a commitment to Jesus Christ to come forward for prayer. I was bursting to go forward, but what would I have to give up to follow Jesus? I had already lost most things: my marriage, home, and old life. Giving what was left to God was not difficult. I needed a fresh start.

Eventually, I peeled myself off the seat and went forward. As the vicar prayed for me, I felt electricity filling my body as I was being filled with the Holy Spirit. Perhaps God was confirming how real he was!

The following weeks were a magical blur. I was now a new creation, totally devoted to this God who loved me, and I was determined to follow him and find all he had for me.

1992-1994

Packing up the house

The next few months were a whirlwind. I had to pack my belongings and leave the home I had expected to stay in forever, with no idea where we would live or how to manage financially.

However, I now had God! I believed He would lead me and take care of my lovely little family. I remained in good spirits and in faith for better times ahead while quietly hoping God would send a miracle cheque through the door and ease my current predicament!

A week or so before we were to be out of the house, the council advised me that they had found us temporary accommodation at a warden-controlled group of small properties where the homeless were housed pending being given a permanent home. We could stay there until a suitable property was found. I was relieved that we didn't have to go into a bed and breakfast but also filled with trepidation. With Georgina at playschool and the others at school, I went to see the lady warden to arrange the tenancy. As I knocked at the door, I felt sick inside, but her friendly manner quickly put me at ease.

'Are you the family moving into number four?'

'Yes. I am here to sort out the tenancy.'

She beckoned me into her office, which was a small room in the front of her house. 'Sit down, and I will make us a cup of tea.'

She went to the kitchen and came back carrying a tray with two cups of tea and a plate of biscuits.

She passed me the plate. 'Tell me your story first, and then I will show you the tenancy paperwork.'

She was so easy to talk to that I told her the entire story of my marriage breakup and losing the house. I could tell nothing shocked her as she listened attentively.

'I expect you hear stories like mine every day,' I said. 'I am so worried about my children and how this move will affect them.'

'Don't worry yourself too much,' she said reassuringly. 'Children are not only more resilient than you think, they also get their stability from you. Provided you stay calm, they will be fine. Try and keep them at the same school, though. That will help immensely.' She added.

Her advice was so encouraging. 'Good luck,' she said. 'Ring me if you need support. Anytime.'

Tenancy arranged, I got on with the daunting task of moving all my belongings. I felt sad to be leaving my dream house, but life was too busy to feel anything for long. I had to stay strong. The children didn't need to know all the difficulties surrounding the move. I was determined to bring them through the ordeal, so I decided to turn the whole affair into an adventure.

With the help of some church friends, we moved into the homeless unit, where we stayed for four months, storing our excess furniture in a friend's barn. The unit was very basic, but it had a small kitchen, a bathroom and two bedrooms. One bedroom was big enough for all four children to sleep in bunk beds. This made it an adventure! They made dens in the bunks and played all sorts of games.

Living in the homeless unit with several families was surreal. There was a Bosnian refugee family in one house where the wife cried non-stop because she'd had to leave some of her family behind. I wondered why the little children from number 6 were always sitting on the front doorstep until I was told that their parents were taking drugs indoors. Noisy arguments accompanied by the sounds of smashing glass were often heard coming from number 8 in the early hours of the morning.

Despite their difficulties, my new neighbours turned out to be nice, straightforward people with no airs and graces. This was such a breath of fresh air after an upbringing where reality was never discussed, and feelings were not allowed. I loved how these new friends were honest and able to express themselves so freely.

Christmas 1992 was hard. I had little money for presents, so I sold some old jewellery to the local jeweller for cash. I also advertised and sold some other possessions through the local newspaper, managing to raise enough money to buy Christmas presents for the children and decorations for the house.

It was a hard time, but we treated it as a family adventure. We were all together, and I remained calm. All would be well.

Moving On

My faith continued to grow during this time, and we regularly went to church and Christian clubs, which the family enjoyed. Hungry for the things of God, I went to a part-time Bible college and attended every Christian event I could. I was learning new ways to live and raise my family, which was benefiting us all.

After four months, we were offered a small but permanent brand new three-bedroom house in the same town. It was a bit cramped, but we squeezed in some of our stored furniture and sold the rest to pay for living expenses. We survived on maintenance payments topped up with social security benefits being just enough to pay household bills and food.

The pressure took such a toll on me that I went to bed tired and woke up tired, dragging myself around like a lifeless mule.

I must have been running on adrenaline during our homeless period. With so much to think about, I had managed to keep the depression at bay, but once we settled into our new home, the events started to catch up, and it soon returned.

The final straw came when a letter dropped through the letter box. I opened it expecting a household bill, only to find it was from the bank, filing me for bankruptcy!

Like a lamb to the slaughter, filled with shame, I went with all my financial papers to see the official receiver appointed to manage the first stages of bankruptcy. He was very helpful. My debts would be written off after three years, and I could start afresh. I could also have a small job to help make ends meet. However, my bank account was closed, and my chequebook and card were no longer valid. Suddenly, I had no bank account and had to use a savings cash account to manage my finances. All non-essentials had to go, and I survived on a weekly cash allowance. The worst part was seeing my name under the bankruptcy section in the local newspaper.

Despite my faith, I was secretly becoming worn out and despondent. Bringing up four children was overwhelming. They needed so many things, including school uniforms, clothes, and shoes, that it was hard to juggle the finances.

Visits to the shoe shop to have their feet measured were a regular event, and I always hoped their feet hadn't grown! One day in August 1994, we were at the local shoe shop, and the five of us squashed together on the long bench seat as we waited for an assistant to become available. It was always chaotic when we went out—the children either pushed and shoved each other to sit next to me or ran to the display to find the shoes they liked.

'Behave yourselves!' I whispered furiously, hoping no one was watching us. 'Put them down! Don't touch that! Come back and sit down!'

Eventually, the young female assistant approached with her shoe measure. 'Who's going first?'

'Me! Me!' Georgina squealed, jumping up and down on the bench.

'I hope their feet haven't grown.' I said to the assistant in a shaky voice. 'I only bought these shoes a couple of months ago. Their feet seem to grow faster than I can keep up.'

'Hopefully not.' she replied, measuring each child's foot one at a time. Then, she pointed at the eldest two girls. 'These two have grown two shoe sizes. You cannot squash their feet in these for much longer.'

Secretly despairing, I knew they needed new shoes for the Autumn term. 'Let's find the cheapest pairs then.' I said, feeling like a failure as the assistant brought the shoes over.

How on earth am I going to pay for food this week? I wondered on the way home. Two pairs of shoes had cleaned out my cash.

I had taught the children to pray, and that evening we sat together in the lounge for a family prayer time.

As usual, Georgina wanted to start. 'Dear God, please bless everyone in the world and keep Mummy safe.'

'Georgina, why do you always have to go first?' her sisters snapped, and a sibling argument erupted.

'Quiet!' I bellowed. 'Everyone can have a turn if you stop arguing and sit still!'

The children quietened down and took turns praying.

Finally, it was my turn. 'Dear God, please provide us with food this week. We have run out.'

The following morning, a food hamper sat on the doorstep, delivered as a promotion from the milkman. What a wonderful answer to prayer!

'Kids, look!' I called. 'We've been left some food.'

They cheered and danced around noisily.

Prayer times were part of our everyday lives, and as God answered, it increased our faith. I prayed for them when they were sick and when we had any need. God never let us down, always providing what we needed, and we learned to trust him for everything.

Church was good, and I found love and acceptance among my new friends. I opened myself up to prayer, found this a great blessing and started sharing more intimately about my struggles. It was so lovely to have friends who could pray for and support me. My faith was growing, and I felt sure God would only lead me into good things.

CHRISTMAS 1994

First bad depressive episode

I tried hard to make a new start, but I was profoundly exhausted, my mood was low, and I couldn't find a way to recharge myself. My mental health soon deteriorated, but I carried on, not knowing what to do about my emotional state.

Every day, I prized myself out of bed, got the children ready, dropped them off at school and then returned to bed until it was picking up time. I had no energy for anything else. As ill as I felt, I was determined my children would not be affected. I struggled along with household chores and getting the children to clubs, with a false smile hiding my torment.

I prayed to get better, but the depression pressed hard on my soul, thoughts, and feelings. When I asked people to pray for me, they were only too pleased to pray, quoting scriptures and words of encouragement, and I kept hoping to wake up the next morning feeling completely better. But nothing worked to pull me out of the emotional and mental pit. As things didn't improve and time went on, I lost hope and fell into an abyss of despair as tormenting thoughts whirled around my mind. It was difficult to sleep for any length of time and I was troubled by nightmares.

June, one of my Christian friends, noticed I was not myself. 'I don't think you are very well,' she told me one day. 'I am really worried about you.'

'I have been feeling like this for weeks,' I said anxiously. 'I don't know what to do.'

'I think you should go to the doctor,' she suggested. 'I will come with you if you like.'

I was anxious about seeing the doctor, scared they would put me on some awful medication, but I was seriously unwell. June made the doctor's appointment for the following day, picked me up and then accompanied me into the doctor's room. My mind had become so chaotic that I barely noticed my surroundings.

The doctor was nearing retirement but had a kind expression. 'Hello, Rebecca.' he said in a soft voice. 'How are you?'

My eyes welled up, and my stomach churned. 'I am not sure what is wrong with me,' I blurted tearfully. 'I can't think straight, my chest is tight, and I can't sleep at night. I don't know what I am doing most of the time.'

June passed me a tissue from her handbag. Having her there was reassuring.

Dr Brown took my blood pressure and temperature. 'Have you been experiencing a lot of stress lately?'

'Yes, over the past few years, but things are more settled.' I replied. The tears ran down my face as I told him about my ordeal, and he scribbled some notes on my medical record.

'You were probably running on adrenaline during the stressful period,' he said. 'This is common when people have been under a lot of strain, but as things settle down, it can all catch up with a vengeance.'

There was silence as he continued filling my medical notes; then he leaned forward in his chair and said words I will never forget:

'Rebecca, you are having a nervous breakdown.' His expression was sombre. 'You will recover, but it could take a long time.' As expected, he prescribed some anti-depressants and sent me home to rest.

He must have said other reassuring words, but I was both horrified and terrified. Realising that I had lost the ability to function properly felt awful. My mind was all over the place, and I found it hard to add up even the most basic of sums. I finally had to admit that I was unwell, and the shame and stigma of having a mental illness made me want to hide. I didn't want anyone knowing about this unless they had to. Having a nervous breakdown and losing the capacity to think straight was terrifying.

The doctor also recommended getting outside for regular walks, which I did, but I continued struggling with even the most basic tasks for a while.

The medication eventually started working, and my old zeal returned, but my battered emotions and mind could no longer cope with any conflicts and pressures. With what little resilience I could muster, I held myself together, still struggling inside. That experience was so awful and frightening. I couldn't let it ever happen again.

After soldiering on for about six months, I came off the medication, not because I was ready, but because of the stigma: I was ashamed to have a mental health problem and wanted to prove to myself and everyone else that I was perfectly fine. Provided I kept a level head with my emotions hidden away, all would be well.

Hurt and bewildered, I stopped going to church. I had received prayers from numerous well-meaning people, yet I ended up in this mess.

Could I even trust God? I had whole-heartedly believed he was good and had a plan for my life, so why did he let this happen?

I decided to take back the reins of my life and forge an independent path. It was best to trust no one and become totally self-reliant.

Thinking all I needed was a career and a future for myself, I applied to a local university to study law. That sounded very important, and I was sure I could do it. I was called in to an interview and offered a place as a mature student starting in September.

I was very pleased with myself!

Another new home

I decided I needed a new project as my mind was very active, and it was best to be thinking about something positive and useful.

Someone wanted to move out of a council house in my old village, and I thought it a good idea, particularly for the children, to return to where we had friends. We looked at each other's properties and decided to swap (exchanging homes was easy in social housing). Several weeks later, the new tenancies were drawn up and signed. This house was a lot bigger, with a large garden, which greatly appealed to me. I was ready for this new phase of my life.

The semi-detached corner house looked old and unkept, but it had great potential. There was a large green area opposite where all the children congregated to play and an old outhouse with a butler sink that was useful for muddy shoes and boots. There was no heating except for a coal-fired solid fuel heater in the lounge, but the lack of central heating didn't bother me; I loved the nostalgia and simplicity of having a real coal fire. It was like going back in time – life would be simpler and easier.

That said, lighting the coal fire was tricky, and I often had to recruit a neighbour to help. Once lit, there was endless piping hot water providing us with long lazy bath nights. Very much appreciated in an unheated house!

The wind would often blow through the old metal windows, moving the curtains, especially at night. The rest of the house had been undecorated for years, and the good-sized but whitewashed rooms needed some colour.

I loved sprucing up our new home with leftover paint and stencils, doing my own thing wherever I could. My moods were up and down but keeping busy focused and stabilised me.

The large garden had been used for growing vegetables. I looked forward to getting out and trying my hand at growing something.

The children loved their new home and being able to play with their friends on the lovely green area outside.

For a while, life was blissful. It was a hot summer, I had a new project, and the children were happy and amused. I even managed some part-time work in order to run a cheap car.

Then, the Christian thing started playing on my mind. I couldn't leave God out of my life forever or stay outside church anymore, so I decided to go to a Christian camp that I had attended before. They were always good, and hopefully, I might find answers to my confusion.

We packed a tent in the car, and off we went in the summer of 1995.

SUMMER 1995

The week my life changed forever

It was a good four-hour drive to the camp. Once we arrived, I attempted to set up the tent. I must have looked quite funny trying to work out which part went where and getting all tangled up in the guy ropes.

Thousands of Christians had come together to seek God and refresh their faith with a variety of seminars by well-known speakers and meetings every day.

It was a safe, peaceful, and loving place for me to find God again, but it took ages to pluck up the courage to attend the meetings. I still questioned why God allowed me to have a nervous breakdown and was unsure whether to trust him with my life. I also had so much pain inside, and I didn't want anyone or anything to provoke it.

But as the event went on, I sensed God's presence. If you have never experienced this, it is the most wonderful thing: a love far deeper and greater than human love. It draws, wows, and fills you with such a sense of peace. There is nothing like it. My heart gradually softened, and I let my guard down.

God's promise to me

I decided to get some prayer and tentatively approached one of the pastoral team.

'Could you pray for me, please?' I asked, ignoring the butterflies flapping around in my stomach.

'Of course.' the man replied, immediately beckoning his wife over.

They put their hands on mine, which felt reassuring, and they asked God to fill me with his Holy Spirit and love. We waited quietly, and then, moments later, the man began speaking.

'God wants to heal you and make you completely whole.' He said. 'If you let him into your emotions, he will take out all the pain and heal you. It will not be easy. In fact, parts of it will be very hard, but as you obey God over a long period of time, all the pain will come out, and you will be totally healed.'

These powerful words broke into my despair and fear. A promise from God that he could heal and *wanted* to heal me? It was a lightbulb moment, bringing me renewed hope.

'I have so much pain inside me that I can't move on,' I told him.

'This is one of the most important weeks of your life,' He replied. 'If you do as God says, he will change you into something so beautiful inside that people won't recognise you.'

It sounded wonderful, but it also left me at a crossroads. 'I am afraid of losing control again,' I said defensively. 'I could never let anyone into my emotional space.'

'Take time this week to listen to God and make your decision.' he said, and they moved on.

I wandered back to my tent. Dinner was beans, tinned potatoes, and tinned stew. I lit the small camping cooker and began to cook whilst the children played. There were great kids' groups at camp, and the children found new friends as they enjoyed the vast outdoor space. I had plenty of time to spend with God, pondering my predicament. I now had so much going on in my head that it was hard to concentrate.

'Dinner!' I called loudly.

We all sat down in a circle outside the tent and ate hungrily.

'How can I ever trust people again?' I said to God, 'And how on earth are you going to heal me when I am such a mess inside? Why did you let me get so ill?' I moaned. 'Why allow me to experience so much pain? If you are God, you should have done something!'

I poured out my heart until it was empty, and there was nothing more to think or say. Exhausted, I slept well that night, snuggled up in a sleeping bag. The next morning, God began to fill my heart with his hope and faithfulness.

Perhaps I could trust him again, I thought. After all, he made me and knows me better than I know myself.

I found myself opening up to a lady called Shirley in the tent beside us as we zipped up our tents.

'What do you think?' I asked, struggling slightly with the zipper on our tent. 'Should I let God do his healing work or keep pursuing my own plans? I know it seems like a strange question. I am used to keeping my emotions hidden and have no idea what shape my healing will take or how long. It all seems very scary.'

Shirley was very kind and wise. She stopped what she was doing and invited me into her tent.

'You need to trust God with your heart, mind, and soul.' She said, handing me a cup of water. 'He won't let you down, especially if he has given you a promise.'

I stared at my hands, trying to blink the tears away. 'But I can't trust people.' I finally said shakily.

'That doesn't matter.' Shirley replied softly. 'God does the healing himself. He will be your counsellor, healer, and deliverer. You simply have to open up to God and trust him.'

Her calming manner left me with a lot of peace, so I thanked Shirley for her encouraging words and left to find the children who had disappeared into their friend's caravan.

As the days went on, I really enjoyed the camp and its loving atmosphere. The week soon ended, and it was time to go home, having made up my mind to let God heal me. This would mean getting back into a church and cancelling my law degree placement because I believed that was not in God's plan for my life. His was a greater plan!

I returned home believing my life would change forever.

The healing begins

The camp experience quickly faded, and life fell back into its familiar swing. However, I had a new course to pursue. I found a new church and looked forward to everything God would do in my life.

I had no idea how my healing would happen, but I trusted and waited.

Then, one afternoon, while on my own in the house, I started experiencing God's peace and presence in a tangible way. My emotions stirred, and I began to cry, feeling pain so deep and unbearable that I thought I would explode, fall apart, or lose control. However, God was gentle and patient with me. Little by little, he released the pain, sometimes when I was alone or in church during worship, like a multi-layered sadness deep inside me. I began to get used to these special times.

The more I trusted God, the closer he came, each experience easier and longer, always ending with an outpouring of healing and peace. The intimate moments were so special that I made space to spend time with him.

My emotions had been a wasteland where I had never known any comfort. Now, Father God, with his healing and peace, was filling and changing me with his love.

I also began hearing him more clearly as he counselled me through some of my difficulties[1]. His voice was not audible, but gentle words would unexpectedly enter my mind and heart. I wondered whether to get therapy, but the truth was that God really had become my counsellor and healer. He was sticking to his word and ministering to me directly. Who could do it better than the Creator who knew me inside out?

It was the beginning of a long, healing adventure. There was more to come, but at the time, God only gave me what he knew I could cope with. There were still a lot of broken parts in my life from my childhood and deep wounds and roots that he would later address.

I entered into a new relationship with God, no longer seeking my own plans but fully committed to his, and studied the Bible through a variety of courses, learning more about God and his faithfulness.

I started reading from Exodus, where God brought the Israelites out of Egyptian oppression and led them to the Promised Land. It was a difficult, often hungry, journey of wandering in the wilderness for the 600,000 Israelites and

---

[1] My sheep hear My voice, and I know them, and they follow Me - John 10:27

their vast flocks. Yet God miraculously provided food (manna) for each day, intending that they learn to depend on him. Yet they continually complained to their leader Moses, claiming they had been better off in captivity. God was not pleased with their moaning, and most failed to enter the Promised Land.

As I studied these stories, I recognised something of myself in these Israelite people. I was on a journey, living in faith was uncomfortable, and I didn't like not being in control! One morning, as I was praying, I felt God say, 'Rebecca, you insult me when you complain'. God was my provider, and to complain was to insult his name and his provision.

He was chastising me to step up into the life of faith and be thankful for his wonderful provision. This encounter ended my moaning, and I found new strength and expectations. God was no skinflint. He provided for me in abundance.

One day after church, a man I hardly knew handed me a twenty-pound note.

'God told me to give you this.' He said. 'He wants you to take your family out for dinner.' (£20 was worth a lot in 1995.)

Amazed, I thanked him for his generosity.

Another Christian friend rang me up one evening. 'God told me you are cold at night,' she said, without preamble. 'I have sent you an electric blanket and some hot water bottles for the children.'

I began to enjoy living in faith. God's provision was amazing, and he always supplied everything I needed.

Instead of feeling abandoned and bereft, I saw how much he loved me and how precious I was to him as he strengthened me and renewed my mind. Others might reject me, but God loved me and would always provide for my needs.

Jesus said: 'Seek first the kingdom of God and his righteousness, and all these things will be added to you'. If I pursued God with all my being, he would be faithful to me.

God gives me the desires of my heart—a farm

As God released my inner pain, I felt him say he wanted to give me the desires of my heart from Psalm 37:4,

> *'Delight yourself in the Lord, and he will give you the desires of your heart.'*

I had always dreamed of living on a farm but never thought it a possibility. Then came a desire to set up a farm in my garden. At first, I thought I had lost the plot; after all, I was living in a council house. However, I soon realised it was God's doing and part of my healing.

One morning, I was digging out the vegetable patch when I heard my name. John, my neighbour, was leaning over the fence beckoning me.

I walked over to him. 'Hello, John, is everything ok?'

'Gillian and I have been thinking,' he said. 'We know how much you love gardening. Would you like the back end of our garden?'

This was amazing! Someone was offering me part of their garden! This is a dream come true! It must be God's hand!'

He pointed to a large area adjoining my garden. 'You can have this whole section here. We are getting too old to maintain it.'

'I would love it!' I said ecstatically. 'I have been thinking of getting some animals. It'll be a perfect paddock!'

'You can do what you like with it.' He said, chuckling. 'I will check with the council and let you know.'

The following morning, he told me the council had agreed and would send him the paperwork to sign. He kindly fenced off the area, and within a week, it was mine. I really felt it was a special gift from God and started imagining how to start my farm.

I decided to start with chickens and began to plan a hen house and pen. John, a great encourager, gave me a stack of old wood.

I looked at the pile. 'How on earth does someone who didn't even take woodwork at school make a chicken house out of this?' I muttered to myself.

Immediately, it felt like God said, 'I am a carpenter; I will show you.'

I giggled, and then I remembered. Of course! Jesus was a carpenter while he was here on earth.

So, with a hammer, nails, and a saw in hand, I let him guide me in building my first chicken house, which went surprisingly well. I worked out how to make a little hatch on the front, with a slope for the chickens to go up into the coop. A friend's husband kindly offered to put the roof together.

The next thing was to buy some chickens and fence off a small area to keep them out of the main garden. Looking back, I don't know how I managed to do all that woodwork.

Hammering posts was hard work, but I figured it out bit by bit. It was so rewarding making everything myself. With God providing whatever I needed, it was perfect and satisfying.

Then came the day to buy the chickens. I piled the children into the car and set off to the farm shop nearby, where we bought eight lovely Rhode Island Reds. They were productive layers.

The children had great fun collecting the eggs every morning. We enjoyed eating them scrambled, poached, and fried. We had omelettes and something we called eggy bread - bread soaked in egg and then fried – which was extremely delicious. But the best of all had to be the beautiful yellow cakes we made from the free-range eggs.

I loved spending hours watching the chickens peck around their pen. It was like a proper smallholding! I began wondering what animals I could get next. I loved goats. It would be great to purchase a milking nanny goat.

It seemed like a wonderful dream, but would I be able to do this in a council house? My tenant's handbook said we might be asked to 'remove pets if they cause a nuisance'. There was nothing about needing permission. Provided the neighbours were happy, all would be well.

I checked with a few neighbours who seemed happy enough, so I went ahead, believing God would not give me something that could be taken away.

I found two nanny goats, Marigold and Buttercup, for sale in the smallholder magazine. One was in milk, having recently given birth. I phoned the farm, and they agreed to transport them to my home. The pictures looked lovely. It was so exciting!

To prepare for their arrival, a gentleman from my church helped me erect a paddock area using wood taken from old palettes. He also found an old shed that was perfectly suited to house two goats. Now, we were ready for delivery.

I had never milked a goat before, so I purchased a couple of goat-keeping books and read them earnestly.

Soon, the day arrived, and the goats were coming. I lay awake the night before, buzzing with anticipation and adrenalin, ready to meet my two new friends.

Suddenly, my two youngest children started jumping all over my bed. I glanced at my watch.

'It's six in the morning!' I whispered. 'You'll wake your sisters up.'

But they weren't going to go back to sleep, so we went downstairs for an early breakfast, got dressed and went down to the garden to fill up the hay bags ready for the goats' arrival. The two eldest girls were not in a hurry to meet our new additions to the family, but I suspected they would enjoy having them once they arrived.

Georgina sneaked upstairs and started tickling her sisters' feet to wake them up.

'Get out, Georgy!' they shouted.

She ran back downstairs, giggling mischievously.

'Come on, girls!' I called upstairs. 'It's time to get up! The goats are on their way.'

They crawled out of bed like a couple of land snails and eventually joined the rest of us.

Nearer the time, they all kept peering through the net curtains, pushing and shoving each other for a front-row view by the lounge window.

'They're here! They're here!' They chorused after a few minutes.

I looked out to see an animal transporter, with two men in the front seat, stopping outside our house. Marigold and Buttercup, a cross between a Golden Guernsey and a Saanen, peered out curiously.

I yanked the front door open and ran outside. 'Is that Marigold and Buttercup? Bring them through the gate over here!' I couldn't help shouting. It wasn't only the children who were excited.

As the men led them through into the new paddock, I noticed that the goats were surprisingly big, the size of large dogs. They looked friendly and placid, and their tails wagged back and forth. They seemed to like their new home. Once safely confined in the paddock, I called the children over. The goats started nibbling at their clothes, which made them all shriek with laughter.

Meanwhile, the men gave me a quick demonstration on how to milk Marigold and then left.

I was now alone with a bucket and two goats. At first, I couldn't get any milk out of the udders, but Marigold was such a good girl. She stood quite still while I pulled and pushed, and before long, we were drinking fresh goat's milk.

The goats gave me so much pleasure. Marigold needed to be milked first thing in the morning and then before bed, but the task was a joy, and I never tired of it. Afterwards, I filtered the milk and put it in the fridge. The milk had cream at the top, tasted good and was perfect for the family. I also made yoghurt.

The goats were now part of our family life, and we have very fond memories of all their antics!

A glimpse of the holiness of God

As God restored my life, he continued with my emotional healing.

After becoming a Christian, I tried hard to get everything right. I had always wanted my earthly father's approval, and this 'striving to please' continued in my relationship with God. I was not aware of it then, but I kept trying to please God by being holy and good. People try to be good, thinking it makes us righteous and holy, but God was about to teach me a fundamental lesson on holiness.

One Sunday morning, during a time of powerful worship in church, I had an encounter with God in which he gave me a glimpse of his holiness. The nearest way I can describe it is being so near to the sun that you get burnt by its sheer brightness and heat. It felt a bit like that. I thought I would die if I saw any more of it. When God's holiness comes near, you can see the filthiness of your earthly nature. I asked God not to show me more, as I was sure I would die in this Presence.

Then, as God asked me, 'Did you think you could ever make yourself holy?' I instantly realised I was rotten through and through. None of us can make ourselves holy in any way. Only God can do that.

I was reminded of the Scriptures. When he had an encounter with the Lord, Isaiah said, *'Woe to me,' I cried. 'I am ruined! For I am a man of unclean lips, and I live among a people of unclean lips and my eyes have seen the King, The Lord Almighty'* (Isaiah 6:5 NIV). I saw myself as filthy and unclean and realised the enormous cost for Jesus Christ to have left the purity of heaven and descended into a world of filth and sin.

After this encounter, I stopped trying to be good and holy. Now, I could cooperate with the healing God wanted to do in me, and with his power leading me, my striving could end. I would be at peace while God slowly refined me.

ANIMAL ANTICS

Goats are fun

Goats are highly intelligent and mischievous. Marigold and Buttercup never missed a trick to get out of their pen in search of a tasty lunch. Natural escapologists, they would find any weak part of a fence and be gone. The neighbours' gardens being prime targets and colourful roses their favourite, beautiful bushes were stripped bare in minutes.

I often found myself wrestling them from neighbouring flowerbeds, embarrassed and, I confess, somewhat amused. Eventually, I trained them to walk calmly on a collar and lead, and the problem was solved.

My characterful goats soon became celebrities among the local children, who frequently came to see them. The adults began to enjoy them, too, now that their flowerbeds were safe. Being sociable creatures, the goats revelled in the attention and grew perfectly comfortable with the locals, especially those bringing apples, carrots, or cabbage leaves.

Very occasionally, the animals were transported by road, to which they quickly adapted, clearly fascinated by the passing scenery.

Healing continues

My relationship with God was growing, and I continued to share my feelings and experience his healing.

I still had bouts of depression and periods of exhaustion where I could not do anything, often triggered by stress or pressure. It felt like just one more challenge, and my mind was on the edge of collapse. My resilience was low, and I became afraid of any conflict or pressure. The doctors prescribed rest, but this was not easy with four young children and a small farm. I finally agreed to try the anti-depressants again. After several weeks, I felt brighter, and my energy resumed. The doctor said I had a chemical imbalance and told me to stay on the medication and give it time to work. My quality of life improved, and my mind and emotions felt stronger. The depressive spells didn't last as long, and my mind didn't collapse at every stress.

God continued with my healing. Sorting out my feelings from my childhood was very confusing. Because it wasn't all bad, my emotions were difficult to understand. Parents can be controlling and harsh but also loving and kind. Talking to friends in similar situations was really helpful. June had also had a difficult childhood, and she had great insight as we talked and laughed and got angry together. We went for walks, coffee and out to the pub, during which we cried and worked through our ups and downs. With these reflections, I started to understand my family's dynamics. The control, lack of emotional support, and witnessing Dad bullying my mother had traumatised me.

Forgiving those who hurt you was a biblical principle I needed to practice with my past relationships. It is easy to say you forgive, but not so easy to do, especially when your emotions are running high. It is also important not to push negative emotions down and pretend they don't exist in a pious attempt to honour God. I worked this through in my own life by deciding to forgive, and I started praying for those who had hurt me. I believe this honoured God. During my prayer times, I was expressive and real about how I was feeling. I gave God all the emotions from the depths of my soul, just like the poetry found in the Psalms. In doing this, I found release and God-given peace.

If I ever found myself ruminating and allowing my pain to turn into bitterness, I stopped myself as I knew this would only hurt my own soul.

Over the course of time, I no longer bore anger or grudges, and I had at last forgiven those who had hurt me from my heart. I loved what God was placing inside me, removing my rottenness, and giving me his love, and I wanted no hindrances.

The depressive spells continued, but now that I was taking medication, they were more manageable. I looked towards the day when God would completely heal me.

Another lady who needs mentioning in this book is Auntie Violet, my mother's sister, a Christian spinster who had never had children. She lived in Cornwall most of her adult life but moved to Essex when my children were small. She was from what I call the 'good old days', with routines that never changed. Monday was Wash Day, Tuesday was for shopping, and Friday was fish and chips day. On Sunday, it was at least two services in church in her best outfit.

Her front door was always open; you didn't need to knock.

'Come in!' she said when I stopped by one day. 'How lovely to see you! Put the kettle on, and we will have some tea.' Her house smelt of flowers freshly cut from her garden, placed in a vase on the lounge table. Her bedroom smelled of lavender, which she put in little fabric bags to keep her clothes fresh.

'We were just passing and thought we would pop in and see you,' I replied, filling the kettle up with water.

'Where are the children?' Auntie Violet asked.

'Georgie's with me, and the others are at school.' I replied.

In her lounge was an old bureau which was full of arts and crafts that the children played with. There was a glass sliding door at the bottom, which, if you opened it, was full of old treasured toys: a small Lego set, some building blocks and two knitted ducks. Georgie ran to the bureau. Auntie Violet had a way of making the toys feel special. No matter how many times she played with the knitted ducks, Georgie never tired of them. In the bookcase was a book called *Nancy the Naughty*, which Auntie Violet read to the children if they had misbehaved. They sat up wide-eyed and listened to her every word.

As Georgie settled down to play, we had a cup of tea and chatted. Auntie Violet was always interested in what we were doing. She listened and offered help and support if needed. She also knew her Bible inside out and always offered a scripture and prayer before you went home. She knew my family dynamics, and I could talk to her about my healing. She was compassionate and understanding and treated me like a much-loved daughter. In turn, she became an important part of my life and healing journey.

The more love God poured into me, the more I changed. The new people in my life showed me what unconditional love was. They didn't condemn me when I made a mistake but showed compassion and forgiveness.

My values and attitudes were changing, and I was becoming a different person. I rejected my father's Victorian attitudes since I didn't want my children brought up without emotional love, unable to express themselves. I wanted them to be loved and accepted.

My parents were now living in the West Country. Although they visited from time to time, and I sometimes went down to see them, I never confided in them about my healing as they would not have understood. I tried to honour them as best I could but inwardly, I was becoming a different person.

Molly the lamb arrives

One day, while buying goat food at the farm shop, I saw an advert that read: *'Orphan lambs needing homes'*. Intrigued, I decided to check it out. I rang the number, and the sheep farmer invited me to pop over, so I dropped the children off at school before heading to the sheep farm.

Lambs become orphans if the mother dies giving birth or has triplets and doesn't have enough milk to feed them all.

I instantly fell in love with the tiny, three-day-old lambs. The farmer, who seemed desperate to get rid of them, showed me how to bottle feed using an old wine bottle and a teat, and before long, I was driving home with baby 'Molly' in the back of the car!

What a surprise when the children got off the school bus to find a lamb waiting for them!

We bottle-fed Molly until she was old enough to go without milk. She became so tame that the children took her for walks on a lead to the garage for sweets. Back in those days, you could move lambs without licenses and red tape. We even took Molly to the primary schools, where she was the star during school assemblies.

Molly also loved being groomed. We brought her into the house for a sponge down, then brushed her with an old hairbrush. She was the best-groomed sheep ever!

Then Molly grew into a big sheep and started to barge down the fences. It was no longer practical to keep her at home, so we had to decide what to do. All smallholders must make the same decision:

'Do I use my animals in the food chain or keep them as pets?'

Keeping every animal as a pet was unsustainable, so after a lot of soul-searching, Molly had to go. If I wanted to increase my livestock, I would have to do what all farmers do and raise them for meat. It was one of my hardest decisions, but part of the learning process of keeping a smallholding.

My relationship with the animals changed after Molly. I no longer named or got attached to those destined for meat.

New Creativity

I found amazing new ways to manage my finances, shopped carefully and discovered new recipes to make food go further. Once upon a time, I would have gone out for drinks and meals. Now, a night out with friends was a bottle of shop-bought wine and a takeaway, but somehow, we enjoyed it more.

Having been encouraged mainly into academia, I had never developed my creative side. At this point, I felt God wanted to release my creativity. I decided to take a free home furnishing course at the local college. In the first session, we all had to make a pin cushion. I was not used to the slow pace and initially found it frustrating to sit there and sew. However, it was nice chatting with the others in the class.

I was pleased with my efforts, so I purchased orange and mint green cotton and made the children's bedding, curtains, and bed covers to match the new décor in their room. The result looked so good with the wallpaper. It was the first of several curtain-making and sewing projects.

It was wonderful to find and develop my creative side. I also enrolled on a flower arranging course which I enjoyed immensely. I picked my own flowers and grass from the fields and turned them into beautiful baskets to decorate my home.

Buttercup has babies

Meanwhile, the farm was expanding. Marigold was providing milk for the house, and it was time to let Buttercup have babies so we would have two milking goats. I had no idea how it worked, but it sounded good to try. She needed a Billy goat to mate with, so I searched in the British Goat Society Handbook, found no end of Billy goats who would be pleased to oblige, picked the nearest one to us and waited for Buttercup to come on heat.

Goats on heat will call out with high-pitched bleats for about three days, wagging their tails restlessly so it is easy to spot. As soon as Buttercup was on heat, I rang the farm, and a Billy goat was delivered within the hour. The keen goat was pleased to be of assistance. After a quick visit, he left.

I will never forget the smell. Nanny goats don't smell at all, but uncastrated Billy goats have a pungent stink that drifts about for days. We waited to see if Buttercup was pregnant.

After some weeks, her sides expanded. I waited patiently as the birthdate approached, planning to be at home when she went into labour. However, Buttercup decided to have the kids when I was out. My eldest daughter was at home, and, with my neighbour, who happened to be a nurse, delivered two kids: one male and one female. What a great surprise when I came home from work!

Buttercup looked after her babies well. We kept the female kid and called her Millie, while the male kid went off to the goat farm to be raised for meat.

Things were going well. The farm was thriving; however, I dreaded a visit from the housing association.

What would they say if they saw the farm in the back garden? Thankfully, apart from the odd workman cleaning the drains, there was never an issue.

SUMMER
1999

A new season and romance

I was quite content with my family and farm and had little time for romance, but God had another plan.

One day, Jed, a young man from the next village, came to a Christian social group I had arranged for single parents in the area. As we got chatting, it became clear we had a lot in common. He was bringing up three children on his own and had kept a goat. We had fun exchanging goat stories, and it wasn't long before we realised we were getting very fond of each other. We did not know what to do. I was living in a council house, and Jed was a self-employed tradesman. We didn't have a house big enough for seven children! Was it practical to pursue our love?

We took our dilemma to God in prayer. Then, I sensed God prompting me to swap houses with Jed's next-door neighbour. I thought the idea was good but could not imagine the neighbour wanting to comply.

We pondered for a while, and I decided to knock on her door and ask! Afraid of looking a fool, I paced anxiously outside her door. It took me ages to pluck up the courage to knock.

The door opened, and a woman called Betty poked her head through.

'Hello!' I blurted out before getting straight to the point. 'Would you consider swapping houses with me? I have fallen in love with Jed, your next-door neighbour.'

Betty stared at me, expressionless. Then, a brilliant smile lit up her face.

'This is amazing!' She said, laughing. 'My sister lives near you, and we've been wondering how she and I could move closer to each other.'

'Really? I am so glad I asked.' I replied, jumping for joy inside and thanking God, both for the idea and for making me brave enough to follow up on it.

'I will come and have a look.' Betty said.

'When?' I asked, still hardly able to believe this was happening.

'Let me sort some things out, and I'll be round later today.'

At around 5pm, there was a knock on my door. It was Betty.

She came in, looked around my house for about half an hour, seemed happy, and we agreed to swap. It really happened as quickly as that!

By now, Jed and I had completely fallen in love and wanted to be together. We shared our love of the good life, our children were similar ages, and although there could be problems, we were confident that things would work out. The children had their own spaces and houses, and God was right in the middle of it all.

Another move

Moving was relatively easy. We did it ourselves, using vans and cars. Our biggest problem was the animals. Would they fit in the new garden? Probably not. We decided to rent farmland nearby so we could both relocate the animals and expand the livestock. It was exciting to put up new fences and move them to an idyllic field overlooking the beautiful countryside. It would be our special space, and we would spend many good times there building our farm and enjoying our time together.

After a busy time moving home, we settled into our new life. Jed and I got married in September 1999, a small, quiet affair. We were too busy bringing up the seven children for big weddings and parties!

Jed had an eight-year-old daughter and two boys, aged twelve and fifteen. My children were now eleven, twelve, fifteen and sixteen. Altogether, we were a readymade youth club! Creating a blended family was full of challenges and change, but with God's help, we managed to deal with the difficulties. Raising them was the number one priority, and much of our spare time was spent running the seven children around to clubs, friends, and after-school activities. Jed worked full-time, and I managed to get a part-time job in the local post office, which fitted perfectly between children's demands and livestock management.

Each child was different, but we enjoyed encouraging and helping them find their way through life's ups and downs.

They are all independent now, with their own career paths. We are so proud of them and really admire each one's individuality.

Married life on the farm

One day, the local farmer, Jeff, called by our land.

'Hello, there,' he said, 'I have a couple of sheep and wondered if you would like them.'

'What sort of sheep?' I asked curiously.

He pulled a white, rather scruffy-looking sheep out from the trailer. 'This one's called Lambchop.'

Lambchop appeared happy to have escaped, bleated loudly, and started eating the grass.

'The other one is called Coco.' he said as a black, long-haired sheep scrambled out clumsily. Coco had long, curly horns but was quite good-looking for a sheep!

'We have not kept sheep before,' I said. 'but thank you.'

'You could breed from them if you want,' He suggested, 'If you bring them back to me for three weeks in the autumn, I can put them in with the ram.'

'Well, thank you!' I said.

We manoeuvred them into a pen with the goats, and Coco and Lambchop settled in well. The field was surrounded by quiet countryside, and we used to take the animals out for a walk down to the river. Marigold, the natural leader, always went in front, and the others followed. Lambchop and Coco loved joining the walk even though they sometimes fell behind as they munched on the lush grass. That autumn, they went off to meet the ram at Jeff's farm. It was all quite easy. When they came back, we looked forward to them having lambs in the Spring. We laughed and imagined the entire landscape amassed with bleating sheep and us rounding them up on horseback, Australian style!

Sheep sometimes need assistance when giving birth; while we hoped and prayed that they would have them when we were present, we often arrived at feeding time to be surprised with beautiful baby lambs! Coco and Lambchop were good mothers, and it was much easier than trying to bottle-feed the orphan lambs.

We continued to breed from our goats and sheep, regularly having lambs and kids in the Spring.

Our chickens were kept at the house so we could keep the foxes away. They were easy to look after – needing a bit of chicken mix, fresh water, and someone to lock them up in the hen house at dusk. One day, someone kindly gave us four little chicks, telling us they were hens. We were only too pleased to take them, and we mixed them with our other chickens, but as the chicks grew, three of them developed large tails, arrogant strides, and a very different voice. They were actually cockerels! They gradually bred with our chickens and produced a whole load of mixed breed hens and cockerels. At one time, five roosters woke the neighbours up every morning at six with their cock-a-doodle-doos!

Eventually, we moved them to the field where they could be as noisy as they liked.

The farm was great fun and everything I had ever wanted.

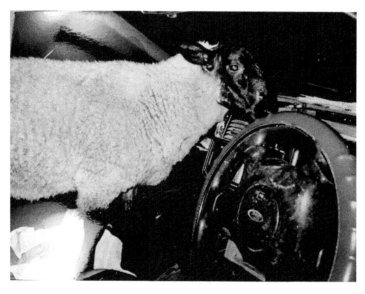

Here is Charlie the sheep anticipating his first lesson in our pickup!

COWS, PIGS AND SPINNING WHEELS

Learning to spin

Keeping sheep involved the annual job of shearing. By the summer, the sheep's thick, woolly coats were hanging almost to the ground, and they were thankful when we took them to the farmer for shearing. It was always difficult to know what to do with the fleeces afterwards. Sadly, most fleeces were thrown away or burned, as they were worth nothing at that time. Fortunately, I discovered a spinning guild that took my fleeces to spin. But there was no monetary market for them.

Then I heard that Ethel, an elderly lady in the village, had a spinning wheel and could show me how to turn my fleeces into wool. This excited me as it would be another step towards my self-sufficient lifestyle. She lived right up the top of the hill next to the church, so one evening, I decided to knock on her door for a chat. Ethel was a spinster who had lived in the same house all her life, inheriting it from her parents. Everyone knew her as one of those people who spoke her mind. If she didn't like you, she would tell you straight!

She peered through the crack in the door. 'Sorry to trouble you, Ethel,' I said. 'I wanted to talk to you about spinning.'

'Spinning?' she said, 'What about spinning?'

'Jed and I keep sheep and often have to throw away the fleeces after shearing. I heard that you spin and wondered if you would teach me.'

'I haven't done that for years!' she replied. 'I'll have to get my spinning wheel out from the back room. I tell you what, come here on Tuesday evenings, and I will show you.'

'That's great!' I said. 'Shall we start next week?'

'Next Tuesday at 7pm,' she said, 'Don't be late!' With that, she shut the door.

It was all set, but I needed a spinning wheel. I checked the local ads, but it was not the sort of thing sold locally! Then I found a shop near London that sold all types of spinning wheels, fibres, and wools. Off we went, thrilled at the prospect of a new project.

When we arrived, I was amazed that a shop like this existed in the 21st Century! They sold a variety of spinning wheels and fibres in stunning colours. It was difficult not to buy everything. Hours later, we left with a spinning wheel and beautifully soft merino, mohair, alpaca, and angora fibres, some of which were dyed in spectacular colours. I looked forward to experimenting with them.

At home, Jed put the wheel together, and I was ready for my lesson.

My first lesson was how to hand spin using a drop spindle, which I found quite hard, but Ethel said was necessary. Lesson two was how to card the wool with two carders, which were like sharp square hairbrushes. You brushed the wool between them, combing it into something usable. Once carded, the wool was ready for the spinning wheel.

Spinning is simply twisting fibres together to make a strong, useable cord. It took ages to get the hang of it, but after several sessions, I managed to produce a ball of wool. I used the fleece from Coco, our black sheep. After several weeks, I finally had a beautiful ball of wool. Ethel was an expert, and she shared with me all the spinning tips she had learned over the years. Having lived in the house all her life, she also knew all the old village tales, which made the evenings really fascinating. It was a privilege to spend time with her.

After much practice, she and I decided to demonstrate our skills at the village fayre, a lovely rural show where many interested folks wanted to give spinning a try.

I continued to spin the fleeces, and it was great making felt from the wool, too. Together with friends, we held craft afternoons, enjoying our newfound skills.

A childhood dream to own a cow

I still had a secret desire to have a cow called Daisy, but never thought it possible, so it had remained a childhood dream. Then, one day, someone mentioned that a farm nearby was selling calves for twenty pounds each, which was not a lot of money for such a beautiful animal. Beef prices had fallen due to an outbreak of BSE[i], which made beef very unpopular.

My ears pricked up, and I wondered if we could buy one. The farm was not too far away, so we went to look. I fell in love with the calves instantly. They had lovely, soft eyes, just as I remembered. Twenty pounds was all it took, and the deal was done!

I was over the moon but needed to sort out transportation. The farmer had offered his horse box to move any animals, but that day, the tyre was flat! We decided to use our people carrier instead. There was plenty of room for the baby cow once we took out the back-row seats.

The journey back from the farm was quite amusing; a cow in a people carrier is an unusual spectacle. We had hoped to go unnoticed, but Daisy was spotted when we stopped at the traffic lights. Her head was facing the back window. The children in the car behind pointed and laughed, the passengers in the car beside us laughed, and the driver honked as they passed us.

Then, just as we were about to pull away, there was a small explosion followed by a smell like a sewage farm. Daisy had pooed all over the back of the people carrier. We had put something waterproof on the floor, but the smell lasted for weeks despite our best cleaning attempts.

Daisy settled into the farm and made friends with the goats and sheep. We fed her a pail of special calf milk and cow mix, and she quickly grew. When she was big enough to graze, a local landowner named Alan said she could share his six-acre field with his horses, which gave her the space she needed.

Daisy was very special. Even if she was at the far side of the huge field, she walked over to greet us whenever we passed by.

Pig Stories

Now I want to tell you about the pigs.

Pigs are probably the funniest animals we have ever kept. They are remarkably intelligent, responding well to human interaction. We often found them playing with a football or having a splash around in the paddling pool.

Keeping pigs was something we had to think hard about. They are not easy to handle. The boars are powerful and can be stroppy, even dangerous. The sows are easier, but both have a reputation for appalling table manners and a less-than-pleasant stink! However, I was determined to give it a try. My motto was, 'Every good farm must have pigs'.

We discovered that breeding them would be difficult – they needed housing inside over the winter, which was not very practical. A fully grown pig is enormous, so we opted to buy small piglets early in the summer and fatten them up for slaughter by autumn. We first tried in 2000 with two Gloucester Old Spots, a ginger one with black spots and the other one pink with white spots. They looked very attractive. We fed them on household scraps and, not being very experienced, let them grow too big and fat.

We kept them outside and gave them a very good life. As well as pig mix and scraps, the local bakery gave us old bread and cakes when they closed for the day, and the pigs enjoyed cream buns and crusty loaves. (Probably why they were so fat!) We took them both to the slaughterhouse, where one was turned into bacon and the other into pork and sausages.

Despite their reputation for being smelly, pigs are quite clean. They did their toilet in one place in the pen, making it easy to clean up. They also loved having a bath. We filled an old paddling pool with fresh water each morning, and the pigs loved getting in for a soak! As they are unable to sweat, this is how pigs cool themselves, along with laying in mud, during hot weather.

After the Gloucester Old Spots, we purchased large white pigs, which were excellent for producing top-quality meat. The only thing was that being outside, they tended to catch the sun, so every morning, I put suntan cream on to stop them from burning. Their morning routine was feed, fresh drinking water, and a nice cold bath. After that, they would have the sun cream on, ready for the day ahead.

Pigs are also excellent for turning over and fertilising the ground ready for growing veg and crops. They spent hours turning the soil over with their snouts, eating any weeds and nettles as they went along. We found this to be a marvellous method of crop management. They disposed of our food waste and were of great amusement to our children and grandchildren.

Pigs need fencing in, which was always challenging as they could get their shoulders under a piece of fence and, with tremendous strength, lift it up and push their way underneath. One day, a neighbour phoned to say two pigs were spotted walking to the next village; and we knew they must be ours. Recapturing them was not easy, but a farmer got them off the main road and put them in a small paddock.

Moving the pigs was another challenge. We were inexperienced at getting them to do what we wanted, so our first attempt to load the grown pigs into the transport took several days. They outwitted our every attempt until we finally found a strategy that worked. Days before moving them, we substituted their housing for the animal transporter by placing their feed in there, which meant they had to go in to eat. After a few days, they used the transporter happily, and we crept up, shut the door, and moved the carrier off with the pigs safely inside.

Going to slaughter was always a sad day. The slaughterhouse had a butcher on site, and you would drop the animals off and collect them days later, ready for the freezer.

The meat was organic and tasty. Our pigs had a great life outside, with lots of space and attention. One pig usually produced an enormous amount of meat, so we filled the freezer with mincemeat, sausages, pork chops, pork loins, pork steaks, and numerous cuts for our large family. Two or three pigs each year would see us through till the next. They were our main source of self-produced meat for years until we no longer needed that quantity once our children left home.

Self-sufficiency

We were producing all our meat and now wanted to produce fruit and vegetables. There was room in the two gardens, so we dug a large vegetable patch and also rented a plot at the local allotment. Fruit bushes were planted wherever there was a space, and before long, we were picking and eating our own fruit and veg. It was hard work, but our dream was to be self-sufficient.

Growing your own veg is not easy, especially if you want to be organic. We had endless battles with black flies on our broad beans, and the caterpillars ate the cabbages overnight. However, we harvested nice crops and delighted in eating home-grown veg grown from seed.

We grew blackcurrants and redcurrants, with which we made countless jars of jam and delicious crumbles and pies. The excess harvest went into the freezer to be consumed over the year.

Next, Jed decided to make his own beer and wine. This was a great success and was consumed by our friends and family. The wine became known as 'laughing wine' for its ability to provide contagious laughter whenever it was drunk! He brewed it in the airing cupboard and had a job keeping up with the demand!

One Christmas, we sat down to our Christmas dinner with pork instead of turkey. Everything on the plate was home-grown. All the hard work had paid off.

A real achievement.

MORE HEALING

Breaking free from family strongholds

Forming and nurturing a new blended family required a lot of personal change. Jed and I had to work out new ways of doing things, with flexibility and open-mindedness, to successfully unite the two families.

My parents were now running a small antique business. They phoned from time to time and visited when they were in the area. In the summer holidays, Mum came up on the train from the West Country to collect the grandchildren. The children loved going, but I always felt uneasy. What if Dad had one of his outbursts whilst they were there? Occasionally I drove down to stay with them for a couple of days and enjoy the lovely countryside. However, I was always on tenterhooks in case someone voiced an opinion contrary to Dad's. My faith, path of self-discovery and life experiences had sculpted great changes in me, but Mum and Dad had not changed and seemed unable to appreciate who I was becoming. Instead, I was expected to line up to their expectations and toe the line as usual.

In 2001, my daughter and her partner announced that they were expecting a baby. We were delighted and looked forward to meeting the new addition to the family. A few months before the baby was due, I drove down to see my parents for a short visit and stayed with my sister, who now lived nearby.

Whilst I was there, I called my mum. 'Do you fancy coming out for lunch or a coffee?' I felt it important to spend some time with her.

'What about your dad?' she said.

'Surely he'll be okay on his own for a while?' I replied. 'We'll only be an hour.'

'I will ask him and ring you back.'

Ten minutes later, she rang. 'Dad says okay, as long as you're not too long.'

I picked her up ten minutes later.

'This is a nice surprise!' She said as she got into the car, but she looked tired with dark circles under her eyes.

It was lovely to have Mum to myself, but she seemed distracted. Over lunch, I tried to lighten the mood by talking about the growing family.

'Dad can't get his head around the baby,' Mum said pensively. 'I have tried to persuade him, but it's no good. He is making a terrible fuss because they are not married.'

'We are really excited about the baby!' I replied, feeling annoyed at her negativity.

Why does Dad have to ruin something good with his condemnation? I thought as I studied her strained expression. *He really is stuck in the Victorian age*! After lunch, I dropped her off at home. It was the last time I would see her properly for two years.

Later in the evening, I drove back home. I liked travelling at night, the roads were clear, and the car headlights illuminated the road ahead. The journey back gave me time to detox from the negative family attitudes that had started rousing old childhood feelings.

As I cruised along the motorway, I longed for the sanctuary of my home. It felt like I was in between two worlds—my parents' world was critical and disapproving, while, in mine, life might not always be easy, but we were happy and didn't judge or condemn.

When I got home, I couldn't hide the fact that I was upset.

'Dad ruins things and puts a negative curse on everything.' I told Jed, failing to hold back my tears. 'I can't go on living between the two worlds. I am a different person now and want to be myself. I don't want to listen to that out-of-date nonsense anymore.'

'Your dad regards himself as the head of the family.' Jed replied. 'He doesn't seem to realise that he relinquished that role when you got married.'

'He still expects things to be done his way.' I said, wiping my tears with my sleeve. 'I can't continue to please him, Jed. I need to be free from his controlling influence.'

In order to grow, I had to confront the control and dynamics operating in my birth family. Little did I know that God was preparing me for a great confrontation and deliverance.

It took three or four days for my mind and emotions to calm down since every visit rekindled feelings of disappointment and despair. But life rolled on with the usual family busyness, and the underlying feelings eventually settled down.

A few months later, our first grandson arrived, and we were over the moon. One night shortly after, the phone rang.

''Hello,' Dad said in his officious voice. 'I wish the mother and baby well. But tell them that I cannot accept the child until they are married.'

Speechless and numb, I hung up as soon as I could.

'Who does he think he is cutting my grandchild out of the family. He isn't the head of my house!' I cried furiously to Jed. 'I am definitely not passing his condemnation down to my children or grandchildren.'

This was the last straw. I really had to be free from his insufferable control.

The party invitation and separation

A few months later, three days before Christmas, my parents held a golden wedding celebration and asked their children to attend. We were expected to drive three hundred miles for a two-night break. The idea was lovely, but it was impossible to find anyone to look after two houses, a farm, and our children. Under pressure all around, I decided we would not attend and wrote a thoughtful note to my parents. I hoped they would understand.

Not so! Mum and Dad were furious, and a series of difficult phone calls took place. They continued to pressure me, but I had to make a stand. Dad not getting his own way was unheard of, and he started with his explosive fits of rage, determined to bully me into submission, but God showed me that Christ in me was bigger and stronger. He gave me the wisdom and strength to manage Dad's behaviour and attempts to control me, which seemed to come from every angle.

Dad eventually realised I would not submit this time, and my place was given to someone else in the family.

It felt like I had escaped at last!

This challenge created a terrible separation between us. Dad wanted nothing to do with me for years, demanding my mother do the same. Deep down, I knew love would empower Mum, and she would fight to see me. However, until then, the rift would remain. At this point, although I didn't know it, I was removed from their will as a punishment. Such was his controlling influence.

Having no parental relationship left me feeling distressed, utterly unloved and abandoned. My moods fluctuated from the deepest rejection one moment to joy at having escaped the family's control the next. Everyone needs a father's love and protection, and I went through a period of grieving for the father I so needed but never had. It felt strange grieving for him when he was still alive, but

God reassured me as I tearfully poured out my anguish to him. He became the Father I needed, and our relationship became closer as he drew me to himself. It was difficult, but God would make it right as part of the healing journey he promised me.

The separation period was a time of great personal growth. First, God delivered me from the control that had been affecting my life. I recall answering an altar call during a church service. The Holy Spirit fell on me, and something that had been oppressing me for years departed. I believe this was the release from a controlling family stronghold. After this, I felt different. For the first time, I could form and express my own opinions without the spectre of condemnation hovering over my soul. I developed new values and beliefs, loved meeting people of different cultures and started seeing the world from a new perspective.

God built in me the resilience and confidence to confront and deal with controlling situations. I was no longer afraid of confrontation. I could now say, 'I don't want to do this,' without feeling afraid or condemned. People didn't abandon, bully, or condemn me if I said 'No', either. I could now challenge something if I felt it was not right. The damaged part of me became my strength as God placed his spirit inside me.

There were no visits to see my parents, but after a couple of years, Mum came to see me and her grandchildren. We tried to talk about the family dynamics, but she was not open to the conversation, and it was swept back under the carpet. It was nice to have her back in my life, and we enjoyed our time together, even if it was only for a couple of hours. The unresolved rift with Dad was not reconciled for nine years, leading to an uneasy truce and polite wooden conversations at family gatherings.

SUMMER 2008

Working at the psychiatric hospital

God had been healing me, and I became very interested in mental health. Now that the children were more independent, I decided to apply for a job at a local psychiatric hospital. The application form was quite straightforward, and I was called for an interview.

The hospital was in an impressive Victorian, red-bricked mansion with large grounds. As I approached the large front entrance, my tummy churned with equal amounts of anxiety and excitement.

I greeted the smart-looking receptionist. 'I am here for an interview.'

She smiled before summoning me into a huge waiting room that looked like something out of a period drama. Long heavy curtains fell in front of sash windows, and the old-fashioned sofas gave the room a rich and opulent feel.

As I sat down, I noticed a lady sitting on one of the sofas, twiddling her hands and rocking backwards and forwards. After a while, a tall, slim man, whom I presumed was her psychiatrist, called her into his office. Soon, I was called before two suited managers. They asked questions, which I must have answered correctly, as I was offered a job starting as soon as the paperwork was completed. A few weeks later, I went for my induction.

An efficient-looking nurse with thick blond hair tied up in a ponytail welcomed me onto the ward.

'My name is Claire,' she said warmly. 'I am going to show you around this morning.' I was quickly introduced to other members of the nursing team who were busy on their computers.

'There are four wards in the hospital,' Claire said, beckoning me to follow her.

'This doesn't seem like a hospital!' I said. 'There are no antiseptic smells, and the rooms are carpeted, with their own ensuite bathrooms.'

'It can seem more like a plush hotel,' Claire replied as she hurried along the ward corridor. 'It's a nice place to work.'

As we approached the adult ward, patients sat chatting in the communal seating areas. Suddenly, a loud alarm sounded from a nearby room. Claire sprinted off, followed by a flurry of nurses running through the corridor. Not knowing quite what to do, I peered through the door. A group of nurses were holding a lady on the bed. There was blood on her face and head.

'Can you go and get the doctor, please?' Claire shouted to me. 'You will probably find him in the ward office.'

'Ok.' I said. As I left for the office, the lady who had been in the seating area pushed in front of me.

'Can you let me out, please? I need to go outside for some fresh air.'

'I am not sure if I should.' I said. 'It's my first day.'

She started pacing up and down, glaring at me.

I managed to locate the doctor who tended to the patient. After a short while, Claire appeared and continued with my induction.

'Life on the ward is always full of action,' she said. 'You have to be prepared for all sorts of emergencies.'

'What happened to the lady in the room?' I asked curiously.

'She was head banging on the wall and smashed her head.' Claire replied matter-of-factly. 'The doctor is attending to her now.'

How awful! I thought. Having experienced the torment of depression, I wondered if her thoughts had become so bad that head-banging was her only way to relieve the distress.

'The lady in the red slippers asked me to let her outside.' I said to Claire.

'That lady is an 'absconsion risk[2]' and would probably have run away.'

I was pleased that I hadn't let her out but pondered on how much there was to learn.

Claire showed me how to observe the patients and gave me a clipboard to fill in. My job was to check on the patients every 15 minutes and record my findings.

'Spend time chatting with them.' she said. 'Try and keep them settled.'

I spent the next few hours chatting and observing patients on the ward.

---

[2] Absconsion risk definitions can include leaving an inpatient unit without permission, entering the community, or escaping during escorted leave, etc.

'Hello,' I said to a lady called Judith, who was resting on her bed. 'How are you feeling?'

Judith opened her eyes. 'Not very good.' She said in a quiet voice. 'Are you new here? I've not seen you before.'

'It's my first day.' I said.

'I've been here for two days,' She said. 'My husband went off with another woman three months ago, and I tried to take my own life. They put me in here. The doctor said I need therapy and a change of medication.'

'I'm sure they will be able to help you here.' I said, surprised at her openness. 'Everyone seems so nice.'

She shut her eyes again as though she was going back to sleep.

'Shall I get you a cup of tea?' I asked.

Her eyes fluttered open. 'That would be fantastic,' she said. 'I don't feel I have anyone in the world who cares for me.'

'What about your family?'

'My mum and dad are dead, but they weren't very nice. I don't have any children. I really wanted some, but it didn't happen. Maybe that's why he went off with someone else.' She closed her eyes again.

That poor woman, I thought, as I filled the kettle in the kitchen. *No wonder she's depressed.* I couldn't help reflecting on my own story. *What would have happened to me had I not been healed and rescued by God?*

When I arrived back with the tea, Judith was getting dressed. 'Thanks for making me tea and for the chat.' She said.

'Why don't you come and chat with some of the other patients on the ward?' I suggested. 'It might cheer you up a bit.'

She put the mug to her mouth. 'I'll drink this first and see how I feel.'

'I will pop back and see you later.' I said before leaving to see the next patient.

In the next room was a man called Ronnie.

'Hello, Ronnie, my name is Rebecca.' I said. 'I'm new here. Just popped in to see how you are doing.'

'I wish you would leave me alone to die.' he moaned. 'You lot insist on helping me, but I have been in and out of psychiatric hospitals all my life, and I have had enough. I've tried every medication going, and nothing has shifted my depression.'

'Maybe they'll find something that will work for you?' I wasn't sure what else to say.

'They want to try me on the ECT again, you know, the Electric Shock Treatment. It helped a bit before, but the depression still came back.' After a pause, he continued. 'I can't see the point of carrying on. They won't let me die, but it's not their life, is it?'

He was so frank.

I could well imagine how he felt after years and years of depression.

'I don't want to put my family through any more. I've not been an easy person to live with over the years.' He added after a momentary thought.

'Don't give up hope,' I told him. 'Maybe it will be different this time.' All I could think about was how God had healed me of so much.

That night, I was exhausted. The shift had been thirteen hours long, and I was mostly on my feet.

'How did it go?' Jed asked.

'I met some lovely people,' I replied. 'They had difficult lives and desperately need some love and care.'

'I am so grateful to God for healing me, you know.' I continued. 'Otherwise, who knows where I would be now?'

My induction day was followed by eight years on the wards. I did the training and became part of the regular staff team. I loved my job and developed huge compassion and empathy for the patients. I desperately wanted to help and tell them about a God who healed broken people.

Mum's brush with death

In November 2010, the phone rang. It was my sister 'Mum is in hospital,' she said.

My heart sank. 'What happened?'

'She started swelling up all over and has been rushed to the hospital in an ambulance.'

'It sounds serious. I will get there as soon as I can.' I promised.

With the children now able to look after themselves, it was easier to get away. After several phone calls, it was agreed that my sisters and I would all drive there and stay with Dad to keep him company. It felt strange going back into Mum and Dad's house. As I pulled up outside the house, I could see him reading at the dining table. He always had his special chair at the head of the table where he ate his meals and read.

'Hello, Dad!' I shouted as I came in the back door.

He looked bewildered. 'Hello, dear.' The television was on far too loud, betraying his deafness.

I noticed he had a dark, lost look in his eyes. Surrounded by his medication blister packs and magnifying glass, he no longer resembled the grand master of the house.

I felt a sudden rush of compassion, which surprised me.

'I am very pleased to see you,' he said. 'I don't like being without your mother.'

I was pleased my sisters were already there, and after a brief catchup, we retired to bed. It felt strange all staying together and we all whispered and chuckled like children.

Early the next morning, the phone woke me up. Grabbing the phone bleary eyed, I was informed that Mum had taken a turn for the worse and we were all to go to the hospital.

I looked at my watch. It was 7:30.

As I put the phone down, a wave of fear and panic washed over me.

Was Mum going to die?

Getting Dad up and out was our priority.

Dad, we have got to get to the hospital.' I said, trying to wake him up. 'Mum's taken a turn for the worse.'

'Oh dear,' he said, sitting up slowly. He looked frail and bewildered.

Dad took a multitude of tablets first thing and was a slow riser. I tried my best to give him his medication, and then I bundled him into the car. Having no idea what to expect, the mood was focused but solemn.

As we followed the signs through the long sterile corridors, there was a disturbing silence, broken only by doctors and nurses hurrying and forcibly pushing through swing doors. Finally, we came to the ward and approached the nurses' station.

'Hello,' I said to one of the nurses who had her head buried in paperwork. 'We are here to see my Mum.'

She stood up. 'She's in a side room,' she said, beckoning us to follow her.

The morning sun shone brightly through the window, lighting up my mother's bed. Mum was wearing an oxygen mask, and her diaphragm was pumping hard to keep her breathing.

'Your mother had a heart attack in the night,' the nurse informed us. 'Something is wrong with her kidneys, and she also has an infection. We are treating her with drugs, but her body is struggling to cope.'

It was awful to see Mum so unwell.

A momentary look of pleasure flashed on Mum's face as we approached, but it quickly changed to stark concern. She must have been wondering why her family was gathering around her bed.

She pulled off her mask. 'Am I going to die?' she asked the nurse who was fixing her catheter bag. 'I don't want to die!'

'I hope not.' The nurse replied, looking genuinely caring.

Mum looked shocked and frightened.

'Let's have one person by the bed at a time.' I said. 'This is too much for Mum with all of us.'

The rest of the family retreated to the visitor's lounge, taking my dad with them. I sat with Mum and held her hand.

Her strength was taken up with trying to breathe.

'Just concentrate on breathing,' I told her. 'You don't need to speak for now.'

Mum didn't want my dad anywhere near her. I could see she felt too fragile to cope with him. Dad was quite frail himself, and we decided that he should go back home and leave us to care for Mum.

Before he left, he popped his head in. 'Goodbye, love.'

Mum pulled off her mask and threw him an angry glance. 'There's something you need to sort out with your daughter Rebecca,' She gasped.

Dad said nothing but looked painfully awkward as he retreated to the door.

'Don't you forget!' Mum growled before replacing her mask.

I wondered what she wanted him to sort out with me. *It's got to be the golden wedding,*' I thought.

Mum was in a critical state and needed firm encouragement to keep breathing. We all decided to stay at the hospital. We were determined to keep her alive.

'This is so unexpected,' my oldest sister said when we were in the visitor's room. 'Mum has been fit and well and easily walks the hills and vales.'

'I know. It is the last thing any of us expected,' I said wearily. 'Let's hope and pray she comes through.'

It was nice to be back among the family again, even if it felt strange. We took turns sitting with Mum in the side room while the nurses popped in from time to time to check her condition. As night came, we wanted to stay awake and decided to sleep between shifts in the visitors' room. The nurses gave us blankets and pillows.

The ward was quiet and orderly during the day, but once the night staff arrived, the patients seemed to get up to mischief. A confused patient called Martha kept coming into Mum's room and calling out, 'Police! Police! Get the police!' as she shuffled around on her walking frame. Our job was to redirect Martha back to her bed. Then there was Teddie, the singer who constantly serenaded Mum, which she thoroughly enjoyed. The commotion kept us entertained, and Mum held on through the night.

The following day, Mum's symptoms subsided; her breathing normalised, and she was able to remove her oxygen mask. We were overjoyed.

Deciding to leave the hospital was hard. It had been an emotional rollercoaster, and I was torn between staying with Mum and getting back home, but I needed to get back to work. After a difficult goodbye, I went to Dad's to collect my belongings.

I opened the back door to find Dad sitting in his armchair, looking very sorry for himself.

'I've got to go home now, so I need to get my things,' I said. 'It looks like Mum will be ok.' I added. 'The nurses said she is much better.'

Dad looked so vulnerable and lost. 'I don't know what I would do if I lost your mother.' He said. 'She has been my constant companion.' After a brief pause, he continued. 'Your mother has asked me to have a word with you about the golden wedding.'

Oh dear, I thought. *I hope there's not going to be trouble!*

'She wants me to reinstate you in the will.'

I was so stunned that my bag dropped to the floor. *They had cut me out of the will?*

'When your mother comes home, we will go and see a solicitor and get it changed,' He added.

I couldn't believe they had cut me out of the will. I was emotionally exhausted, and this news was hard to take. Stunned all I could offer was a polite goodbye.

I reflected on Dad's words during the drive home. Mum would never have cut me out of her will unless Dad forced her. I imagined the fight she would have put up to stop him from dishing out such a Victorian punishment. I was also grateful to God for healing my mum and using her illness to turn Dad's heart. It must have been part of God's plan.

It took me weeks to recover from the events, and it was particularly difficult living so far away and not being able to see my mum. She gradually became stronger and was allowed home ten days later.

Reconciling with my parents provided peace and a step in the right direction, but I was a different person now. I no longer tried to please my father, and he couldn't control my life. I had changed, and my reactions were now a mystery to him. I was back in the family pack but no longer subservient to the alpha male.

After such a difficult time, I had many thoughts and emotions to process and continued experiencing bouts of depression, often crying out,

'How much longer before you have finished healing me, Lord?

2011
ONWARDS

A home of our own

As time went on, the children grew up and moved away one by one. With only two children left at home, it became impractical running two houses, so we bought a lovely house in the country, finally having a home to call our own. Behind us was wild meadowland, which we rented. We transferred our animals and had them living with us.

Now that the demands of family life had eased, Jed and I held a rededication of our marriage vows and went on a fantastic belated honeymoon cruise to the Canary Islands thirteen years after our wedding. Life was easier, and we could give more time to our self-sufficient lifestyle.

I continued to work in the psychiatric hospital and became a well-respected member of the nursing team. Wards were becoming increasingly busy, and staff were overstretched. I became more and more aware of the patients' need for pastoral support and care and approached the management about setting up chaplaincy and pastoral care in the hospital. They responded positively and gave me the necessary support. It was such a privilege.

After networking with local faith organisations, I managed to install some volunteer chaplains onto the wards. My additional role was now chaplaincy and pastoral care coordinator, and it involved going to the wards, visiting new patients, and telling them about the chaplaincy support. I spent hours sitting, listening to, and praying with patients from all sorts of backgrounds. Some were abused as children, resulting in dysfunctional behaviour. Then there were those who knew no other way to deal with their internal pain and anguish than to harm themselves. I saw people so depressed that they would rather die than continue living. Many were tormented by voices and anxiety, which made them afraid to go out, while others with eating disorders restricted their diets to the point of death. I heard the most awful stories of such difficult lives that it was no surprise that someone could break. I saw people totally overpowered by addictions. I was certain they needed a saviour, and that Jesus came for each one.

Not everyone with mental health problems is in hospital. Many are in our communities. In October 2016, I set up a charity called Replenish UK to offer pastoral care and befriending support to those struggling with mental health problems in the community. Referrals quickly came in from the community mental health teams and others, where services were stretched, and people desperately needed support. This step was an enormous stretch of faith but has gradually grown and continues to flourish.

In August 2017, I left my role at the hospital to concentrate on developing the ongoing work of Replenish.

Mum and Dad's final years

As my parents aged, visiting them became increasingly difficult. Their physical deterioration was apparent, but the dynamics between them was unchanged.

Poor health forced them to spend more time together at home, emphasising a discordant existence, and I invariably left after each visit, feeling upset yet powerless to help. I longed to spend time with Mum, but she couldn't separate herself from my dad, who, as time went on, suffered from Alzheimer's, angina, and poor mobility. Mum became weaker with age, eventually having dialysis for failed kidneys. I visited as often as I could, but it was not easy with the distance. As they approached the end of their lives, I desperately wanted them to know that Jesus could give them eternal life. Mum was open and had committed her life to Jesus when she was younger. Dad resisted the gospel and could not accept that he had ever done anything wrong. Despite my attempts to discuss faith with him, I invariably went home frustrated.

Eventually, his Alzheimer's worsened, and he was sectioned and detained in a psychiatric hospital. Visiting made me dreadfully sad. There was my own father, struggling to uphold a measure of dignity among confused, lost and thoroughly broken souls. The air they breathed was a quietly terrifying fusion of fresh flowers, medication, and urine.

The last time I saw him alive was on a flying visit. I went to the hospital, where I manoeuvred him around the pleasant grounds in his wheelchair. It was a lovely sunny day in July, and I sensed God's tangible peace. A faint smile showed in Dad's drowsy eyes, indicating his pleasure at being in my company. As I parked the wheelchair under a tree, the sun cast shadows on us through the branches as we sat together.

Perhaps he will now understand his sin and need for a saviour. I thought, fishing out my Bible to read him Psalm 51.

Have mercy on me, O God, according to your unfailing love; according to your great compassion, blot out my transgressions. Wash away all my iniquity and cleanse me from my sin. For I know my transgressions, and my sin is always before me.

Against you, you only, have I sinned and done what is evil in your sight; so, you are right in your verdict and justified when you judge. Surely, I was sinful at birth, sinful from the time my mother conceived me. Yet you desired faithfulness even in the womb; you taught me wisdom in that secret place.

Cleanse me with hyssop, and I will be clean; wash me, and I will be whiter than snow. Let me hear joy and gladness; let the bones you have crushed rejoice. Hide your face from my sins and blot out all my iniquity.

Create in me a pure heart, O God, and renew a steadfast spirit within me.

His eyes were shut as I read, then, as I neared the end, he opened them and started praying to the Lord God Almighty. I sensed the Holy Spirit was touching him.

'Is there anything you need forgiveness for?' I asked him.

He nodded. 'Unresolved conflict.'

Dad had fought endlessly with various people over the years. He now wanted to make his peace with God and others. I prayed that God would cleanse him and forgive his sins. And as we sat together under the tree, I gave thanks to God as I knew my dad was forgiven and would be with God for eternity.

The following month, he died in his sleep. I was at peace knowing he was now with the Saviour.

No one was surprised that Dad had died, and the family quickly arranged a funeral. Shortly afterwards, I travelled down to take my mum to the florist to arrange for a beautiful spray to be placed on his coffin. The next day, Mum fell and died from a bleed on her brain. Devastated, the family cancelled Dad's funeral, and a double funeral was arranged in its place. As I helped carry Mum's coffin into the church, it felt like I had carried her to Jesus, where she would be at peace. They were buried together in a cemetery in the West Country.

Mum had taken communion shortly before she died. I am reassured that she is in heaven, and I will one day see her again.

After their deaths, I went through a time of grief and adjustment. I also found tremendous peace and rest from the cycle of trauma I experienced after my visits.

However, there was a cavern of pain deep within me that, when triggered, left me crying endlessly. God had done so much in my life, but I was not fully healed.

GOD COMPLETES HIS HEALING

A mother and father's blessing

One day in March 2018, I was spending time with God, crying, and pouring out the deep sadness within me.

'Why do I still feel like this, despite everything you've done in my life?' I asked.

Suddenly the Holy Spirit stilled my heart. 'Despite the love I have shown and sent you, you lacked love and nurture from your mother.'

At first, I was shocked by this revelation. I had always been quite protective of Mum and didn't like the thought of her failing me in any way. I used to imagine spending time with my mum and longed for her emotional support, but Dad took up so much of her attention that she could not give us one-to-one time or nurture.

I wept at this heart-breaking truth; then I felt the Holy Spirit wanted to give me a message from my mum in heaven.

I guess you can see everything you have done when you get to the next life. Most of us hurt and inflict pain on others, not deliberately, but through a lack of understanding and sensitivity, and I believe this happened with Mum. On earth, she could not see the damage to my life, but all things are exposed in the light of God's glory.

'Hello, Becky, love.' I heard her say. 'I am so sorry, and your father is sorry too.'

I wept like a baby.

'We want you to do everything you want in your heart. Don't worry about a thing.' She said. 'We didn't do our best for you, but we want the best for you now. Go and be all you want to be. We have put our signatures on this blessing in heaven, and God has put his stamp of approval on it.'

In my mind's eye, I saw a written scroll containing these words with Mum and Dad's signatures and God's red seal and stamp over my parents' signatures. It was a mother and father's blessing, something I never had, which would now make a big difference in my life. What could not be done in this life was done in the next and relayed back to me by the Holy Spirit.

I was moved by this amazing visitation from God. I wrote down what I heard and sat basking in God's peace for several hours.

After this, I was filled with a joy I had never experienced before. Living with a parental blessing was wonderful. Their affirmation gave me peace and confidence in my identity, value and worth.

I thought this would bring the depression and sense of abandonment to an end, but I inevitably found myself there again.

'When will you heal me completely, God?' I cried out. I knew there must be more to come!

The following year, I had a heart attack and had to rest. For the first time in my life, I had to be still. God was preparing to remove the depressive root from my life.

The root is finally identified

In February 2020, a friend invited me to a healing event. When I arrived, a mature man who had sought his own healing over a period of many years was teaching. I listened attentively and found the teaching, particularly about something he called 'Trauma A', to be helpful.

He explained that we were created to receive love from God and others; and need lots of love to function properly. If we are neglected, or when good things are held back, that absence wounds us at the deepest level; and that lack of love can be worse than inflicted harm. As he spoke, I sensed a real conviction in my heart. I will never forget him saying, 'Trauma A is the inconsolable cry of a child who desperately needs love that is withheld and never comes.'

This was the root of the endless pain and depression from which I had longed to be healed.

On this life-changing day, God touched and spoke to me. At last, there was a name for what I experienced: Trauma A, the cry of a child from whom emotional nurture and support had been withheld. The cry was so deep that the wound reopened whenever she was misunderstood or rejected in her adult life.

At the end of the healing event, there was time for prayer. As I stood with others, the Lord ministered his consolation, comfort and healing deep into my soul so that the wounded child was comforted and healed.

After that, the sense of abandonment left, and the tears and depression became a thing of the past. My reactions to events have changed, and I believe I am now healed.

FINAL THOUGHTS
ON HEALING

My healing took years. God takes his time and deals gently with us. The process cannot be rushed since he is working with our minds and emotions, both of which are fragile and precious yet must be renewed for healing to take place.

There are many layers of pain, and like an onion, each layer must be peeled back and removed before God finally exposes the root. This was probably the most painful part of my healing. Without my heart attack, I may never have reached the place of rest that granted him access to this part of my life. We can be busy and run away from those things inside us, but God used it all to complete his deep work in me.

Some of my healing has been, as described, during intimate, emotional times with God. Little by little, over the years, the pain inside me has come out. I cried so much that heaven must be filled with my tears.

Some healing has been talked out with friends; I have done a lot of talking!

Some healing came during intense times of deliverance from oppression and childhood strongholds. There have been many prayers and times of release.

I have spent many hours reading the Bible, taking Bible courses and discovering the God who created me. These helped in healing my mind, as well as in my restoration.

Much of it has been the painful realisation of my own weaknesses and need to change. There have been necessary confrontations with my parents and family over the past. Nothing has been easy, but it has been worth the struggle to find this wonderful God-given healing and peace.

Most importantly, healing is a work of inner holiness, and God has required my cooperation and submission.

The restoration and rebuilding that God carefully planned out have been amazing. He gave me the desires of my heart - a farm, a self-sufficient lifestyle, and a new husband to share it all with.

He has brought many people into my life to help me on my journey. He has never let me down.

A WORD ON MEDICATION

Many people take mental health medication, and there is no shame in taking it. It is just like taking a pill for any other bodily depletion like thyroid and diabetes.

God gave us doctors, scientists, and medication to use wisely and well. Medication is part of the treatment for mental illness and sits well alongside faith and healing as part of a holistic model of health and wellness.

My personal experience is that medication helps. Some people experience side effects, but these settle after a while. Prior to being on medication, my depressive spells lasted for weeks. Once on the medication, they only lasted for days and were far more manageable. Medication does not take away the pain and distress, but it makes you stronger and able to cope with sorting it out. It can take a while to find a medication that works. Some people can come off their medication, and some may need to take them long-term. There is no shame in this.

Stopping medication is a common reason for being admitted to hospital and should never be done without medical supervision.

I am so grateful to God that he has healed and levelled out my emotions, so I no longer experience the ups and downs. It has taken a long time, but I am very different. It has been hard, but, having come out on the other side, I can now tell others that God really heals.

The journey demonstrated that there is nothing God cannot do to bring healing and wholeness into a person's life. If you are struggling with internal pain and brokenness, Jesus loves and died for you. Trust him to heal you.

Not everyone realises that God desires an intimate and emotional connection with them. He can come into your emotions to heal and cleanse you from hurts and pains if you give him permission.

If you want God to come into your life and begin a healing work in you, here is a prayer:

> ***Father God,***
>
> ***I acknowledge that I need emotional healing. Please guide and show me your path to my healing. Make me whole and bring me the fullness of life that you promised.***
>
> ***In Jesus' name,***
>
> ***Amen.***

If you do not know Jesus Christ as your Lord and Saviour, here is a prayer to start you on your journey:

> *Lord Jesus,*
>
> *Thank you for dying on the Cross to set me free from my sins. I am sorry for the wrong things I have done. I ask your forgiveness and now turn from everything I know is wrong.*
>
> *Please come into my life, fill me with the Holy Spirit and be with me forever.*
>
> *Thank you, Lord Jesus.*
>
> *Amen.*

Please find and connect to a local church. They will help you on your journey.

EPILOGUE

My story ends in 2024. Life is pretty good. My emotions are stable, and I no longer experience bouts of depression. It has taken years, but I am glad that I waited patiently for God's healing. I felt like giving up and doing life my own way at times, but he always encouraged me to keep going forward. I feel greatly blessed and thankful.

Life on the farm is better than ever. Our children have families of their own, giving us many grandchildren to enjoy. We still keep goats, cats, and chickens and grow our veg and fruit.

There may be another few chapters to write, as God is never finished with us. I look forward to more of his goodness.

My life was broken, my emotions a wilderness of pain and death, and I did not know who I was. God didn't just patch me up. He took me on a healing journey, always restoring me to the person he created me to be. None of my circumstances could stop him from blessing my life.

Jesus said, '*I have come to give them life and life in all its fullness*' (John 10:10).

A FEW VERSES THAT HELPED
ME ALONG THE WAY

"Do not be anxious about anything, but in every situation, by prayer and petition, with thanksgiving, present your requests to God. And the peace of God, which transcends all understanding, will guard your hearts and your minds in Christ Jesus."
Philippians 4:6-7

"Trust in the Lord with all your heart and lean not on your own understanding; in all your ways submit to him, and he will make your paths straight."
Proverbs 3 5-6

"For I know the plans I have for you," declares the Lord, "plans to prosper you and not to harm you, plans to give you hope and a future."
Jeremiah 29:11

THANKS AND DEDICATIONS

My greatest thanks go to Jesus. Without him, I would not have a story to tell.

My thanks go to my husband for his encouragement and creative help in writing this book.

While working in a psychiatric hospital, I was privileged to meet many people with stories to tell. Thank you for sharing your lives and inspiring me to share mine.

I dedicate this book to everyone longing to find wholeness and peace.

To those labelled with disorders and long psychiatric anomalies, this book is for you. There is a God who loves you and can restore you. Nothing is too difficult for him. It might take a while and might not be easy, but he is willing and able to do it.

May God bless you and bring you hope, peace and freedom.

Rebecca X

ⁱ Also known as mad cow disease, BSE is a fatal brain disorder found in cattle.

Finding Freedom will change lives!

However, most of the people who need its message will not be looking for the book. To change their lives, put a copy in their hands. Do not leave it on a bookshelf. Pass it on to someone who needs it.

Printed in Great Britain
by Amazon